650.13
T

DISCARD

T

Tame Your Terrible Office Tyrant™ (TOT)

Tame Your Terrible Office Tyrant™ (TOT)

How to Manage Childish Boss Behavior and Thrive in Your Job

Lynn Taylor

WILEY

John Wiley & Sons, Inc.

Published by John Wiley & Sons, Inc., Hoboken, New Jersey.
Published simultaneously in Canada.

Limit of Liability/Disclaimer of Warranty: While the publisher and author have used their best efforts in preparing this book, they make no representations or warranties with respect to the accuracy or completeness of the contents of this book and specifically disclaim any implied warranties of merchantability or fitness for a particular purpose. No warranty may be created or extended by sales representatives or written sales materials. The advice and strategies contained herein may not be suitable for your situation. You should consult with a professional where appropriate. Neither the publisher nor author shall be liable for any loss of profit or any other commercial damages, including but not limited to special, incidental, consequential, or other damages.

Author's Note: TERRIBLE OFFICE TYRANT, TOT, TAME YOUR TERRIBLE OFFICE TYRANT and logo are trademarks of Lynn Taylor and are used under license.

Individuals, companies and products are mentioned by their real names in this book and related marketing materials for purposes of information and commentary only, and no affiliation, endorsement or sponsorship is claimed or suggested. All other individuals, companies, products and other particulars in this book are referenced with fictitious names, locations and descriptions, and any resemblance to real persons or products is coincidental.

For general information on our other products and services or for technical support, please contact our Customer Care Department within the United States at (800) 762-2974, outside the United States at (317) 572-3993 or fax (317) 572-4002.

Wiley also publishes its books in a variety of electronic formats. Some content that appears in print may not be available in electronic books. For more information about Wiley products, visit our web site at www.wiley.com.

Library of Congress Cataloging-in-Publication Data:

Taylor, Lynn, 1957–
    Tame your terrible office tyrant (TOT) : how to manage childish
boss behavior and thrive in your job / by Lynn Taylor.
        p. cm.
    Includes index.
    ISBN 978-0-470-45764-1 (cloth)
    1. Managing your boss. 2. Executives—Psychology.
3. Interpersonal relations. I. Title.
    HF5548.83.T39 2009
    650.1'3—dc22

                                                2009004147

Printed in the United States of America.

10 9 8 7 6 5 4 3 2 1

Contents

Acknowledgments

IT HAS BEEN a thrill to make this seven-year passion become a reality. The ability to help others through my workplace perspectives and experience, while providing some levity, is a true privilege.

Along the way, I have been supported by wonderful colleagues and friends. Special thanks to Andrea Hurst and Judy Mikalonis, my agents, for their savvy guidance; Lauren Lynch at John Wiley & Sons, Inc., for publishing this book; Mark Butler, for his sage publishing advice and expertise; Wendy White and Christi Williford for their graphic design talents; Helene Williams for her editing; Blake Loosli, illustrator; Jonathan Kirsch, legal/publishing guru; and Ellen Neuborne, Hiyaguha Cohen, and Irina Averkieff for their valuable insights and input.

Thank you to the following people for their contributions: Mary Ellen Gross, Luci Sheppard, Debbie Snow, Betsy Steiner, Mickey Freeman, Helen Kennedy, Colleen McManus, Elijah Star, Kerstine Johnson, Stephen Bonser, Carolyn McCall, Becki Clague, and Jacqueline Rubasky. I am also grateful for the bosses who mentored me throughout the years—especially those who helped me navigate through my own occasional TOT behavior!

I owe special gratitude to my parents, Norman and Homa, for their ongoing enthusiasm, and to Scott, Sue, Gordon and Lori for their support. Last but not least, thanks to Drew, for his spirited wit and participation, and Zack for his constant interest. As young boys, Drew and Zack taught *me* a lot about toddler training. Their joy and youthful exuberance led me to an invaluable principle: let the child inside *inspire*, not rule us, whether in or outside of the office!

Introduction

THERE ARE GREAT BOSSES, and there are terrible bosses, but there is no such thing as a perfect boss. No one expects a boss to be perfect, of course, but the problem is that many, if not most, people get stuck having to deal with those less-than-ideal managers. So what can you do to solve this dilemma?

After working in corporate America for 20 years, and more than half of them with companies that help people find meaningful jobs, I decided to step out to find my own passion in a way that would be personally fulfilling.

I began typing a list of what mattered to me most professionally and how I could contribute to society. I quickly realized that nothing in my own professional career would be more rewarding than to provide employees with tools and shortcuts on getting ahead.

I wanted to share my insights and experience with people to help them advance in their careers, but I knew that I had to offer some humor along the way, too.

And suddenly, it all came together. I had often joked that some bosses were just like little kids, but it soon occurred to me that it wasn't just an off-handed quip . . . it was true! I had discovered my passion: helping workers better understand their managers by seeing the "hidden child" behind the often-frustrating behaviors of their supervisors. I saw striking parallels between troublesome bosses and toddlers—and not surprisingly, the solutions were frequently very similar as well.

At that point, the Terrible Office Tyrant (TOT) was born.

It was a natural outcome of having parented two boys, remembering vividly my babysitting and toddler-rearing days—and having "lived" and researched workplace behavior in various executive capacities. On reflection of my own corporate experience, I realized that I had unknowingly applied parenting techniques in the workplace for many years.

This "parenting" was never done in a patronizing way. Instead, I tried to put myself into my boss's shoes. I looked for the raw, childlike motives behind their actions and personality traits, both challenging and endearing: the characteristics that comprise a TOT. Then I quietly applied the basic discipline techniques that worked most effectively with young kids.

Once I started charting how this notion worked so incredibly well in the office, I knew I had to validate my premise by researching toddler behavior more thoroughly. I talked to or videotaped more than 100 people, and independently commissioned surveys of thousands of others over a seven-year period to confirm the parallels.

The feedback was overwhelmingly positive. In fact, everyone I spoke to responded with a hearty laugh, and some version of: "Oh, I could give you tons of material!"—followed by a personal story.

Shortly after analyzing the whining, fearful, stubborn types of toddlers, I had the harsh realization that I, too, had at various times been a TOT. The more I considered the similarities between TOTs and toddlers, I realized that almost all bosses behave this way at some point. Now it was time to synthesize the solutions to the many varieties of bratty bosses and little lost lambs of the corporate world. I felt that in doing so, I could help make the workplace much more productive.

It was and continues to be a great journey.

Now, this phase of my work is done, but my adventures into the TOT world continue. I envision this as a reference guide for employees at any level who encounter one of the 20 traits outlined. I hope it will offer a "Levity Lens™" through which to view TOTs, not only in the workplace, but also in one's personal life.

My hope, too, is that CEOs will allow the book to proliferate among the ranks of corporate managers. The results will be a more humanized workplace and enhanced profitability, creating a win-win for employees and management. Tips for CEOs are at the end of the book.

I believe that whether we're two or fifty-two, we all have the same core emotions, desires, instincts, and yes, training needs. Each day, we have the opportunity to proactively manage the TOTs around us. By adopting a calm, rational, and professional approach at work, I believe you'll contribute to your own career advancement, and maybe even create a more manageable workplace for others.

I hope that *Tame Your Terrible Office Tyrant: How to Manage Childish Boss Behavior and Thrive in Your Job* will help you see that the corner office is just a palatial playpen—and that you won't let the pinstripes and pearls fool you for one minute. With the ideas from this book, your human instincts, and corporate savvy, I believe you'll be able to add "TOT tamer" to your many accomplishments.

Getting Started: Advice for Employees

GETTING OUT OF BED and dragging yourself to work can be a chore even if you have the world's greatest job. But if you've been hitting the snooze button repeatedly before hitting the shower, there may be something—or more likely, someone—making you want to avoid work.

If your boss acts like a bratty bully or a confused little lamb—or just seems impossible to deal with, you can now breathe a sigh of relief. You are working for a Terrible Office Tyrant (TOT) and help is on the way.

TOTs aren't really any different from toddlers. And fortunately, once you can see that the tyrants are really just wearing training pants, that cell phones are just pacifiers, and that the conference room is just a playground, your work life will be easier to handle.

Using a "Levity Lens™," to see the silly side of the awkward and stressful in the office, can show you that the little devils at work are just playing sandbox politics. And once you understand your boss's quirks and strange behavior, you may not even need the snooze button. That's where *Tame Your Terrible Office Tyrant (TOT)* comes in.

All bosses, just like the rest of us, have vestiges of childlike behavior in them—some more than others. And that means your boss will invariably show a sign or two of being a TOT. In other words, for you to succeed and thrive at your job, you need to become a TOT tamer.

Please note: That's TOT tamer, not TOT kicker, or TOT torturer, or any other aggressive (or arrest-worthy) monikers. The whole point of TOT taming is to "manage up"—not to get revenge on your boss, or to fight fire with fire.

You might want to think of TOT taming as a kind of parenting, minus the diapers and spitting up. Despite the lack of icky and sticky that only a toddler can offer, you still face tantrums, fear, confusion, name calling, and more in the corner office.

After all, your boss is human, too. We all have the same basic human instincts and needs. As in life, putting yourself in the other person's shoes, listening carefully, and reading between the lines often makes a world of difference. Your boss is probably dealing with many of the same challenges that you are—and then some.

Remember, TOTs have bosses, too (aka Big TOT, not to mention Big TOT's boss, Super TOT) who can make their lives miserable. Sure, you have deadlines and goals to achieve, but so does your TOT—who is responsible for the performance and deadlines of everyone on the team.

The tricky part about your boss's management weaknesses and slip-ups is that you have to be sensitive about the way you address them. You can't yell at your boss, or yank a problem away from her and say, "No, no, no, no! We never do that!" as you would with a toddler. But just like a good parent, you can reinforce positive behavior and turn mistakes into a learning experience.

That may sound like going above and beyond the call of duty, but a little TOT taming can go a long way toward reducing angst on the job. And remember, if you aren't someone's boss already, you probably will be someday.

So, how do you become a certified TOT tamer? Use your good judgment, anticipate problems, stay calm and personable—and develop creative, professional solutions. Be acutely aware of your boss's needs and be prepared to dig deeper. Ultimately, you will be rewarded for great results, meaning faster career advancement.

A stubborn boss probably doesn't enjoy being—or even intend to be—stubborn, for example. She may just not have any other tool available to cope. If you can uncover the bigger issues that trigger TOT behavior, you might be able to solve the current problem and head off future ones as well.

Keep in mind that not all TOTs are tamable. You should never have to put up with abusive behavior, or a boss who takes advantage of you and your work. Those kinds of bosses actually transcend TOTdom—and qualify as evil. You should spend your time, energy, and creativity on getting out of that bad situation, rather than trying to fix it.

You don't have to be your boss's best friend to be a TOT tamer or adopt a suck-it-up mentality, either. But your relationship with your boss doesn't have to be contentious. It can be professional, productive, and respectful. Life's too short to live in fear of your job. *Tame Your Terrible Office Tyrant* can help.

I

Bratty Behavior

TERRIBLE OFFICE TYRANTS (TOTS) are at their most terrible when they behave like all-out brats. When your boss morphs into monster mode, you can count on a bad day . . . or a bad week.

Some of the most striking parallels between toddlers and TOTs are, well, also the most obnoxious. A boss who wants a report "Now!" bears an uncanny resemblance to an unruly little kid in the supermarket candy aisle.

A child who bullies others because he's bigger and tougher can be seen in a manager who constantly reminds his team "who's in charge." And yes, both TOTs and toddlers can pitch a whopper of a tantrum, although unfortunately, your boss isn't as likely to throw himself on the ground and cry. (One can dream, though!)

Like small children, bosses like to get their way. That often involves acting out in ways that you thought were limited to little kids faced with a plate of vegetables or the threat of no more video games. To make things worse, a petulant TOT, unlike a child, has direct authority over your livelihood. That's when Bratty Behavior is no longer just annoying . . . it can be life changing.

By understanding what's behind the bluster, you can usually tame your TOT—or at the very least, mitigate unpleasant situations. You might sometimes feel inclined to fight fire with fire, but all that does is get you fired. So be creative and "manage up" when the Terrible Twos appear in the corner office.

Inside this section of *Tame Your Terrible Office Tyrant*, you'll learn how to recognize the telltale signs of an impending brat attack—as well as how to deal with one. Each chapter includes a look at how TOTs and toddlers act out in common, a real-life story about how an employee like you dealt with a challenging boss, and a set of helpful TOT Taming Tips.

1

Bragging

About Bragging

IT'S A BIG DAY in the office because the CEO is dropping by. You've not only worked 24/7 for the past three weeks to cut marketing spending as much as humanly possible—but you've also prepared a detailed presentation, even cleaned the office, and made snacks for all the head honchos.

Now your Terrible Office Tyrant (TOT) saunters in with Big TOT (his boss), and, the CEO. You can't believe your ears. In under 30 seconds, your TOT has taken credit for the reduced budget, the slide presentation you slaved over, the office's pristine look, and—oh no, he didn't—your snicker-doodles?

Before you can register your disbelief (or even introduce yourself to the CEO), your glory hog TOT has planted the big boss in his office—and snagged all of the treats to boot. During the closed-door session, you hear phrases like: "When I saw we could cut . . ." and "Then I thought of an amazing, much cheaper way to achieve . . .," punctuated by loud praise from the CEO, "Excellent! You are running a tight ship."

By the time they emerge to go eat sushi, it's hard to believe you even exist. Your boss has taken credit for everything. In fact, he's painted himself to be the only functioning asset in the office.

"Yikes," you think, "He'll claim he invented the Internet by the end of lunch."

But Why?

What just happened here? You realized that your boss is either the Most Powerful Man in the Universe—or the Biggest Hype in Town. When it was showtime at your office, your boss blew his own horn—at everyone else's expense.

Self-promoting TOTs are everywhere. It's a common trait in the working world, especially when the need to sell goes into overdrive. Talking yourself up is necessary, but, of course, there are some TOTs who escalate self-promotion, trying to elevate themselves above the rest of the world.

Often, their behavior has no ill intent—this kind of TOT simply wants attention or validation. For the most part, bragging bosses are more of a nuisance than a threat. Sometimes, though, TOTs deliberately put down others to bolster their own egos—or ensure their perception of worth in the eyes of their TOT. Like kids who shout, "Your painting is stupid, mine is better," the worst of the blustering bosses leave a trail of hurt feelings and ill will in their wake. Even then, it's still more hot air rather than an egomaniacal power trip.

Let's look at the parallels between braggart bosses and kids who sing their own praises:

Bragging Toddler Behavior	Bragging TOT Behavior
He brags to his preschool classmates, "Teacher is my friend and not yours."	He brags to anyone within earshot how tight he is with the new CEO. But their only encounter was at a meeting where the CEO asked him to take notes.
She scoots down the slide 49 times, yelling "Watch me! I'm the fastest!" after every turn. If you fail to take note and applaud, she screams, "Mommy, watch me!"	In order to "teach" public speaking skills to the staff, he shows a DVD of his speech to a youth group 49 consecutive times. He stops the video frequently and says, "Let's watch again!"
When no one is looking, she draws crayoned circles all over the living room walls. She pulls you into the room. "Look!" she crows. "Best circles ever!"	Your boss grabs the client proposal you just completed. Her edits: adding the word "maybe" to every bullet point, weakening your pitch. She boasts that she transformed it into "a work of art."
Your toddler tells his little sister, "I can hit the ball over the fence and you can't. Na na, na na na."	You challenge his decision to take over a project that requires your specific skill set. He says, "I'll take the lead on this baby." You swear you heard a "Na na, na na na" at the end, too.

Mild gloating is usually tolerable. We all have egos and a little positive self-promotion can be a boost. Bragging only crosses the line when the frequency or volume gets ratcheted up—or when reality starts to distort.

You may find yourself wincing every time your boss struts in your direction to name-drop his many "connections" up the corporate ladder, not to mention politics and Hollywood.

You may cringe when the laundry list of notable career achievements gets further inflated, thinking: "Wow, if he won 'Employee of the Year' as often as he said, he must have started here in kindergarten—or maybe he's actually 112 years old!"

But your irritation might finally morph into fury when his boasting comes loaded with poisoned arrows aimed your way—or even worse, when he claims your accomplishments as his own. That's the point at which you have to stop tuning out your TOT, and start building a defensive shield.

(For help dealing with true center-of-the-universe TOT behavior, check out Chapter 7 on *Self-Centeredness*.)

Bragging begins in late toddlerhood and is a normal developmental stage. The child learns she can do something new, and her excitement spills over into what sounds boastful, but might simply be celebration.

When she says "I made the picture," she's displaying pleasure and enthusiasm in her discovery that she can create something. And when she compares herself favorably to her peers—"I'm bigger/smarter/prettier than you are"—she's working out exactly who she is. She doesn't necessarily want to make others feel small and ugly—she just hasn't discovered the harm her words create nor does she have the capacity for empathy yet.

Most kids figure out early that nobody likes a show-off, so they learn to temper their boastful behavior, but only after testing it. At some point, kids learn that more frequent or louder boasting works even less effectively than regular bragging. They dial it down and keep the big boasts in check.

"Tell Me I'm Great!"

TOTs who brag like toddlers have never resolved their identity issues or developed a capacity for empathy. They also have never figured out that most people want to crawl under a rock when listening to them.

Most likely, they didn't receive enough reassurance growing up, and so they're still seeking it. They brag in order to find out if you actually do appreciate or respect them. They need to hear, "Yes, you are the most brilliant negotiator on the crew," because at age seven, they didn't hear "You are the best kickball player" often enough. The trouble is that many braggart TOTs seem to have an endless need for reassurance, and you can't make up for their childhood deprivation. (Check out Chapter 19 on *Neediness* for more ideas on dealing with deprived TOTs.)

The problem increases in competitive situations, where the TOT feels threatened. He fears looking bad next to colleagues, so he tries to convince you that he's better than they are, and better than you are.

True TOT Tales

Par for the Course

Selma works for a small computer software firm in Denver. If her boss ever heard a rumor that he was a big braggart, he'd probably freeze in his wingtips from surprise, because the behavior has become so ingrained. Here's Selma's story.

> My boss has no shame. He's a big golfer and a bigger showoff, and I'm sick of hearing him cock-a-doodle-do about how great he did in his latest game. He sneaks out at 4:00 PM every Wednesday to play golf, which annoys me because I'm working 14-hour days just to keep my job intact. Then he justifies it by saying he makes all these great connections, and that golf is "integral" to his sales numbers.
>
> Thursday morning is when the golf gloating starts. I know nothing about golf, but he makes me listen anyway. Then, in the

usual "the golf course is my office" riff, he goes on about the deals he clinched and who he bonded with the day before. I know deals get done over golf, but the thing is, my boss has not landed one client from these outings!

This week, he came in beaming. He was especially psyched because he had golfed with a "key guy" from a Fortune 1000 company. He said we'd be a "shoo-in" for a big deal because they talked for hours and "literally hit it off."

Later, as I dropped off a file on his desk, I noticed a scribble on a piece of paper mentioning that same Fortune 1000 company and the next golf date. It turns out this new golf pal was a "Management Trainee." Wow!

I never called him on the fact that no business ever came in as a result of his networking acumen. But I started to use the inevitable weekly boss visits to get his sign-off on my ever-growing list of pending projects. I learned that I could get a lot done with one secret phrase, "How was your game?" Granted, I had to endure a bunch of sand-trap stories, but he became so agreeable that I'd wrap up work before anyone else. I actually learned about golf because of that. But I'm still skeptical about golfers.

Although Selma couldn't escape her boss's bragging, she was able to harness it for her own use. Fortunately, her boss didn't stoop to boast at her expense. He didn't put her down for not having a fancy club membership or for being not being "connected" like he is—he just wanted an admiring audience.

TOT-Taming Tips: Bragging

There are only so many times you can listen to tales about how your TOT impressed all the honchos of the universe with her charm and wit. Though you may understand why your TOT puffs herself up, she'll probably strain your patience after a while, particularly if she points out the many ways in which she surpasses you.

How can you survive the braggadocio in your office? Here are some tips to deal with the blowhards and the windbags at work. In fact, they may be the best tips ever. (Okay, now that's bragging!)

 DON'T DO THIS ...

Encourage a Brag-Off. Let your TOT know that there are other TOTs out there making bigger and better claims than she is. Tell her, "Boss, when the customer service manager heard you say that our team was the greatest team ever, she said that her group was the greatest times two. And then the regional sales director said they were the greatest 'times infinity.' So I said you'll face off with them in the conference room at high noon."

Do This ...

Help Dial It Down. Your boss truly might not be aware of the impact her competitive bragging has on others. You can let her know in a gentle way by saying something like, "It's great news about your high score on the management aptitude test, boss. You're amazing. I do think poor Ron was devastated when you said that you smoked him. I hope he isn't too bummed out. Maybe you could give him a word of encouragement?"

 DON'T DO THIS ...

Crow Louder. It's essential that you establish yourself as the smartest, fastest, coolest employee in the universe, so that you get promoted when the time comes. Adorn your office with every diploma you ever earned, including your dog's certificates for most-improved fetcher. If you find yourself in a room full of TOTs trying to out-boast each other, walk into the middle and say, "Oh yeah? Bet you didn't know I invented the FruitSharpener—the first pencil sharpener that emits fragrance! And a guy from IT said that I visited more web sites while working than anyone else!"

Do This . . .

Model Compassionate Behavior. Reign yourself in when you have something to boast about—and gently show your boss the friendly way to shine. Instead of making a big deal, keep your accomplishment to yourself and later, take your boss aside. Say something like, "I didn't want to make a fuss about getting nominated to the President's Circle because I didn't want Randy or Joanne to feel bad. They've worked so hard, and are good team members, so I'd rather keep this low-key." Hopefully, your boss will follow your example instead of jamming her achievements down everyone's throat.

 DON'T DO THIS . . .

Be Your Boss's Publicist. If your TOT drones on about his accomplishments at every opportunity, help him get sick of hearing it himself. At every chance you get, brag for your boss in front of him before he launches into his own song-and-dance: "Did you know that my boss has the highest IQ on the tenth floor?"

Do This . . .

Hold Up a Mirror for Your TOT. Clearly, your boss thinks that bragging will impress the flunkies or influence the Big or Super TOTs, or he wouldn't keep at it. You can help him learn discretion by pointing out another bombastic TOT. After witnessing a display of egotistical ranting from that TOT, look at your boss and say, "Gosh, you'd think that she'd know the top brass hates bragging. That's too bad."

 DON'T DO THIS . . .

Pump Up the Volume. The next time your boss starts singing his own praises, break out the headphones and rock out to your favorite music to drown him out. If he's still there by the end of the song, ask, "Are you done bragging yet?" and if he says "no," repeat until you get a "yes."

Do This . . .

Be a Fan (within Reason). It can be irritating, but as long as your boss doesn't put you down as she builds herself up, try to table your annoyance. She really does need the pat on the back if she craves acknowledgment and praise to such a ridiculous extent. So tell her she's great and you appreciate her, at least once in a while. You might occasionally reserve the extra praise to reinforce positive behavior at the same time: "I'm so honored that you always value my feedback, boss, and that you want to share your accomplishments with me. I feel that whatever you accomplish, so do I. Thanks."

TOT-Busters Q&A

Question

My boss, Ned, drops names like crazy. When he goes to the doctor, he comes back and tells us about how famous his doctor is. His lawyer is famous, his neighbors are famous, and famous politicians sit next to him at benefits. He has a booth at a famous restaurant run by a famous chef. Now the menu includes "Ned's Duck L'Orange." I'm sick of it. How can I tell him to stop it or stuff it (Ned, not the duck)?

Answer

First try the indirect approach: "You must enjoy being around so many famous people." It might cause a moment of self reflection. But if not, try a diplomatic, yet direct approach. Tell Ned that you like him for who he is and what he does, not for who he knows—you value his leadership more than his speed-dial, in so many words. You'll probably have to repeat the message, but you might eventually hit a chord. Nonetheless, you may have to tolerate some celebrity gossip.

Points to Remember

- Bragging is generally more of a nuisance than a threat.
- When TOTs brag, it's often because they need validation from others to feel convinced of their own abilities.
- Competitive braggers often don't recognize the destructive impact of their comparisons and putdowns.
- Learn to tune out or tolerate braggadocio.
- To redirect a boastful boss, help her to recognize how she hurts people when she elevates herself above them.
- Gently teach your boss that boastful behavior nets no friends.
- Praise your boss within reason.

2

Bullying

About Bullying

IT'S TIME TO OVERHAUL the inventory system, but Al, your Terrible Office Tyrant (TOT), needs sign-off from a very senior TOT (Super TOT, Mr. Kraus), in the forbidden office on the top floor. Al has been mumbling about getting it done for weeks now, but still hasn't acted because he's afraid. You see, Mr. Kraus hasn't taken a vacation for 49 years and it's made him a nasty soul.

You encounter your boss, Al, one afternoon at the candy machine, and then he has a brainstorm. You can almost see the sparks flying out of his head as he glares at you—and the crooked smile blooms on his lips.

"I've got a great idea," he says, "I need you to go up to the 119th floor to get a signature for me on that inventory thing."

"But boss," you say, "Mr. Kraus won't talk to me. You know he won't meet with anyone below senior management level. I'll get disciplined for even approaching his office."

Undeterred, your boss continues, "What are you, a mouse? A chicken? Well then, cock-a-doodle-DO it!!! I don't care how, but you'd better get on task right away—or you'll get disciplined for not approaching his office. Don't come back without that signature!"

You quiver. You suspect that Super TOT will chew you up and spit you out from the 119th floor window, but, on the other hand, your very own TOT is always looking for an opportunity for a good fight. Now he's set you up for humiliation, and if you don't move forward as he suggests, he could fire you. You feel like a kid who's been dared to jump off a ledge.

But Why?

Office bullying comes in many flavors and intensities, ranging from mild manipulation to outright terror. It's one thing to be occasionally told that you need to improve your writing skills, but quite another to be told the same thing three times a day with a threat attached.

The good boss says, "I'd like you to work on improving your reports. Proofread everything and remember to use spell-check." The bully TOT says, "If you don't start writing better-looking reports, we're going to move your desk next to the freight elevator. That way, it'll be easy to dump your stuff out in the parking lot."

Perhaps your bully TOT harasses you about the tiniest details, making you tremble every time you approach once-simple tasks. Maybe she gets you to do her bidding by humiliating or ostracizing you.

The bottom line is that she wants to get her own way, and if she can use you to achieve her goals, she will. If not, she'll push you out of her path. And because she has the power to hire and fire, she has you over the barrel, just like the beefy neighborhood 10-year-old boy, who has all the other scrawnier kids paying a toll just to cross the street.

Paying the toll one time may be okay—you can survive that—but if it becomes an everyday affair, you need to take action.

If you have a truly vicious boss who continually harasses you and undermines your self-esteem, then you need to either quit, or get help from an organization such as http://bullyinginstitute.org or www.bullybusters.org. It's important to note that despite the humorous tone of this book, workplace bullying is no joke when it becomes persistent and destructive.

Bullies at any age share many of the same ruthless behaviors:

Bullying Toddler Behavior	Bullying TOT Behavior
Your toddler leads his sibling outside and holds up a worm. "Eat it," he says. When the sibling refuses, he adds, "I'm telling Mommy you stepped on her glasses. Eat it!"	Your boss tells you to monkey with the departmental figures in the fiscal report. When you balk, she says, "I'm sure you don't want my boss to find out that your team is below target this quarter. Fix it!"
He charges full speed at a much smaller kid yelling, "Vroom, vroom, vroom! Get out of my way or I'll crush you!" When the smaller kid fails to move, your child rams into him and knocks him over.	At the trade show reception, your boss pushes you out of the way, nearly knocking you over, to introduce himself to the CEO of your biggest account. He gives you the evil eye when you greet the CEO, and later scolds you about "protocol."
Your child yells, "Doo-doo head, doo-doo head" at a neighbor kid. When the kid yells back, "You're a doo-doo head!" your child rides his bike right up to the kid and stops 3 inches from his face, towering over him.	"Are you stupid?" he asks when he discovers that you e-mailed a report to the project leader instead of to everyone on the project team. "Or just plain lazy?!"
Your toddler gathers with the other hardened four-year olds in the cul de sac. When a smaller kid makes a bad throw, he joins in with the other kids who yell like a pack of wannabe-hoodlums.	Your boss calls you into the conference room where a gang of TOTs is seated. "Did you make this mud, I mean coffee?" your boss asks as the others snicker. "Pulease—go to Jerry's Java for real coffee!"

Watching kids on the playground, you might think there's a bullying gene. Why else would there always be that one tough kid who torments the smaller ones to get his way? And why, in so many corporate offices, is there the one manager who disciplines employees by badgering, isolating, or insulting them publicly?

Experts say that bullies act out because they learned the behavior from someone else. Maybe they lived with harsh parents who yelled, hit, or intimidated them, and so they emulate what they saw at home, never outgrowing the pattern.

With TOTs, perhaps a mentor or supervisor pushed them around early in their career, and now they're following suit. Whatever the source, the bully thinks that terrorizing weaker people is the proper way to deal with anger and frustration.

Because the corporate structure does give bosses authority over staff, some bully TOTs think they have the right or even the responsibility to intimidate. Also, they lack the vocabulary or tools to communicate their needs and frustrations in a more civilized manner.

The big problem is that once bullies act out, they tend to get results, and so they repeat the behavior. This convinces them that they are really powerful, which gives them a little boost, and so the pattern continues. You have to find a way to break that cycle or get yourself out of that job, fast.

- -

True Tot Tales

Travel-Agency Travails

Suzanne worked for a travel agency, where a bullying boss ruled the roost. As she learned, taming a TOT is sometimes impossible, so she booked a ticket far away from this toxic office.

When I first began as a trainee at a travel agency, Ruth, my supervisor, seemed like a friendly, approachable person, but within a few days, her inner bully really came to the fore.

Since I had no agency experience, I didn't know the online system—or how to fill out the reservation paperwork properly. Ruth walked me through everything, but she talked really fast and had nothing written down. She seemed to think that I would learn instantly. So after her lecture, she told me to start doing ticketing.

Every time I made a mistake, Ruth hit the roof—and I made a lot of them. She literally would scream and call me incompetent. If I asked a question, she'd say, "I thought you were smart. What's your problem?" She'd tell me how much business I was going to lose for her, and she had made a mistake in hiring me. And this was after only a few days on the job.

After a few weeks of this, I started to have panic attacks before going to the office. I worked up my courage and told Ruth that she didn't need to yell at me, and that it was normal to make mistakes when learning something new. That really set her off. She ranted nonstop for 15 minutes.

I honestly don't know what her problem was—if she had a chemical imbalance, or if she just thought that screaming was the way to get employees to pay attention. Her business was very successful, so she had managed to treat her customers nicely enough. In any event, I stood up in the middle of her tirade and told her I had had enough, grabbed my purse and walked out. I never regretted doing so.

- -

Quitting was the best option in that circumstance, since there was nobody above Ruth for Suzanne to enlist for support. On the other hand, if Ruth had shown any signs of being reachable, or if her bullying had been limited to occasional bursts of frustration, it may have been worth a try to manage up and address the situation directly—or at least develop a work-around.

TOT-Taming Tips: Bullying

Remember: a bully wants to get his way, and using threats and abuse is the fastest route to achieve his desired results. That's the bottom line.

Transforming a TOT's bullying behavior takes courage and persistent effort on your part. It won't work with every bully, but, with some, it can be done. If you can show him that he can get what he wants by using gentler, kinder tactics—or that he can earn respect by doing so—you just might see changes. It takes a true TOT Tamer to deal with a bullying boss.

Here are a few tips on handling one of the more troublesome types of TOT:

 DON'T DO THIS . . .

Filibuster Your TOT. If your boss badgers you, fight back with a long, drawn-out response. Describe, in great detail, every nuance of emotion that his behavior evoked in you. For instance, "Boss, when you told the board that my presentation reminded you of a zombie on valium, I noticed a slight, rather erratic twitch in my left eyebrow that gradually traveled down to my mandibular fossa. At that point, it occurred to me that I was experiencing something akin to incipient irritation, at which point . . ." Continue until you have used every adjective in the dictionary to convey that it gave you a funny feeling. Take your time . . . you need about 90 minutes to make the proper impression.

Do This ...

Keep Your Message Short. When your boss bullies you, it's important to tell him how his actions affected you. Ask if you can have a minute of his time and politely confront him, making sure you're concise and serious. Jot down your talking points to organize your thoughts, keep a matter-of-fact tone, and limit your discussion to a few minutes at most. Stick to the topic, and use "I" statements rather than "you" accusations. In other words, don't say, "You made me feel terrible because you used inappropriate language." Instead, say, "I felt hurt after the meeting. Hearing that I gave a boring presentation really stung me."

 DON'T DO THIS ...

Ignore, Ignore, Ignore. Completely dismiss your taunting TOT. One way to achieve total detachment is to blow out your eardrums so you can't hear anything that your TOT says. Go to the nearest construction site, borrow a hard hat, and use a jackhammer while a worker is on lunch break. Go back to work, and let your boss rail away while you remain unaffected. If you don't work near a construction site, you can try Plan B—faking it. Pretend to mishear whatever your boss says. If she snarls, "A monkey could do better," tell her, "Thank you! It really is a funky sweater, isn't it?"

Do This ...

Intervene Early. Pay close attention to early warning signs that your usually mild-mannered boss is about to turn into a big bully. If you know your boss resorts to bullying under stress, try to minimize the stress factors. Has he had a bad day? Postpone unnecessary meetings until the coast is clear. Was he pushed around by his Big TOT or by a client? Lend a sympathetic ear. When in doubt, if you notice a warning sign, get out of the way. Just as you shouldn't stick your face near the snout of a snarling dog, you should remove yourself from the path of a growling TOT until things cool off.

 DON'T DO THIS . . .

Fight Fire with Fire. Make your bully back down by letting her know about your own power. Threaten to steal her stash of chocolates. Taunt your bully boss by asking, "What are you gonna do about it?" If she still doesn't back down, get ready to run, because a real fight might break out shortly thereafter.

Do This . . .

Use Positive Reinforcement. When a TOT who sometimes resorts to bullying treats you with respect, thank her for her kindness. Tell her how she inspires you to work hard whenever she's positive and polite. Become a role model of good citizenship yourself, displaying unwavering courtesy to your boss. If you have to, overdo it to send the message. Never act like a bully in response to bullying.

DON'T DO THIS …

Enjoy the Pain. When your boss gets angry and starts bullying you, bow down and say, "I'm not worthy, I'm not worthy," touching your hands to his feet. Keep a running inventory of all of your faults and submit it to your TOT with suggested punishments for each violation. Barge into the board of directors meeting and start chanting, "I've been very, very bad. Big boss, you need to punish me!"

Do This …

Garner Support. If your TOT truly is out-of-control, bordering on abusive, seek assistance from coworkers and other managers. You need support through this process. If confronting your bully boss directly is not an option, go to a higher-level manager or a human resources manager and present your concerns. Be honest, and be prepared to give examples of your TOT's abusive, bullying behavior. It usually takes more than one person to topple a bully but, with outside support, you have a chance.

That being said, if your boss has taken bullying to a level where you find yourself getting sick with anxiety or depressed on an ongoing basis, you've got a serious problem. It may be time to visit your favorite online job board.

TOT-Busters Q&A

Question

My TOT bullies me almost daily. He comes to my cubicle and chants the same thing over and over again: "Why isn't it done? It should have been done. It better get done!" Can't I just say, "Stop ranting, it saps my motivation?"

Answer

You'll never get a bully to stop by asking, unfortunately. Quell his anger first by acknowledging or validating what he is saying: "you need this work to be done today (or tomorrow or 'in X time')." Mirror back to him what he wants. Then tell him what you reasonably can accomplish: "I'll have it done by 3:00 PM, so it will definitely be done today." Once he is calm, make constructive suggestions to avoid this situation in the future: "Could we set deadlines together on the next project in advance? Then I can be sure to deliver the goods when you expect them."

 Points to Remember

- Bullies learn their behavior from early role models.
- The corporate structure sometimes seems to support bullying, because of the built-in power hierarchy.
- Bullies often lack alternate skills for handling frustration or anger.
- Address your bully TOT in a concise, calm manner.
- Model polite, respectful behavior.
- Reinforce kind behavior from your boss.
- Never bully a bully back.
- Enlist support from colleagues.
- If your boss is consistently abusive, leave your job.

3

Demanding

About Demanding

YOU'VE HAD A to-do list a mile long all week and, finally, just before the staff meeting on Friday afternoon, you're about to check off the last item. You imagine the stunned admiration of your boss, who had to know she asked for the impossible—and the barely disguised envy of your colleagues, who gave you two weeks in this job, tops. That's when your phone rings and the familiar chant of your Terrible Office Tyrant (TOT) nearly ruptures your eardrum.

"My office. Now!"

What could she possibly want? You mentally flip through the litany of recent demands and know that you've addressed every request, no matter how random. But, that penetrating tone in her voice didn't sound like you were about to hear praise for any job well done.

You jog down the hall to the door of her office. Before you can knock, you hear her growl, "Get in here!"

"Those primitive bar graphs you sent over need to be redone. I can't send this garbage upstairs. They'll think I have something to hide. What were you thinking?"

"But . . . I followed the examples you gave."

"Don't 'but' me. You're on thin ice. Just fix it. Now!!!"

You realize that the kudos (and the stunned admiration) aren't coming—and neither is that prized 5:30 PM departure for the weekend. Nothing is ever enough. You might as well be asking a pushy three-year-old to recount all the nice things his mommy does for him when all he can think of is, "why can't I eat all that frosting?"

Why isn't "thank you" in her corporate vocabulary? Does she suffer from memory loss? Doesn't she see that the bar graphs are actually very good—and just a tiny part of a brilliant package you have been working on all week?

But Why?

Much like a toddler, your TOT believes she is the center of the universe—and with the gravitational pull she exerts as your boss, you are stuck in her orbit. Asking nicely doesn't naturally occur to a small child. After all, crying got great results in the early days. If other loud, insistent behavior like yelling or repeating demands worked before, he'll expect it to work again.

Your TOT may not resort to pulling on your sleeve to get your full attention, but, as you might imagine, he's got a few other tricks up his sleeve—just like a three-year-old:

Demanding Toddler Behavior	Demanding TOT Behavior
Your toddler expresses every need as an urgent demand: "Thirsty, thirsty, thirsty!" "Dolly—want my dolly!"	Everything has the same level of urgency to your boss. Due dates for the year-end financial report and ordering that engraved calculator are both ASAP.
She starts loud—and gets louder—if her demand isn't met immediately. "I need my blanky. Blanky! WAAAAAH!"	When your TOT needs something, he evolves from regular e-mail, to ALL CAPS e-mail, to an in-person barked-out order.
A five-minute trip to the supermarket turns into a half-hour wish list recital—in full whine. "I want that! And one of those! Hungry!"	Your boss will hand you a new "mission-critical" project before you've had a chance to begin work on the one he brought by this morning.
Reminding him that you've given him plenty of toys already works about as well as reminding your puppy that your shoes are not his toys.	Reminding your boss that you've put in a ton of overtime will elicit remarks about your lack of loyalty and your inability to "take the heat."

Demanding behavior may stem from a need to control, an inability to empathize, a desire for perfection, or a plain old sense of entitlement. Whatever the root cause, one thing is sure: a demanding TOT is a bottomless pit, and you're fighting a losing battle if you think you can get him to give you the recognition or slack you think you deserve.

You need to adjust your expectations and learn to speak his language. "That's all. You can go," may be demanding TOT-speak for, "Great job. Why don't you go home early?"

Although it may be helpful to your TOT taming endeavors to know that this trait usually begins in childhood, it would be career suicide to point this fact out to your TOT. And besides, the TOT isn't interested in self-examination—especially when there are lots of orders to hand out and plenty of people around to blame.

A "Gift" from Big TOT

Demands don't always begin with your TOT. The original orders may be coming from Big TOT or even Super TOT in the corner office—and your TOT is simply handing off the workload and relaying expectations to you. Since a demanding boss is seeking approval from his demanding boss, the pressure trickles down to company employees.

It may not make you feel any better (and it won't make ridiculous workloads and deadlines disappear) but it's helpful to know that your boss is often feeling pressured by unrealistic goals set by authoritarian Big TOTs or Super TOTs. Working for a slave-driver is never easy. But knowing this helps you survive your TOT's onslaughts—and reminds you not to take it personally.

Not everyone who has power abuses it, but those who do are usually covering up a lot of insecurity. These demanding TOTs are often trying to elevate their self-esteem, much like a schoolyard bully who intimidates others. (See Chapter 2 on *Bullying* for more related information.)

True TOT Tales

Planning Uneventful Events

Sam had just started a new job in Miami as an event planner—a job that had enough demands without a perfectionist breathing down everyone's neck. But Christy, Sam's boss, was a Type A TOT, who brought her own set of demands to the party:

> From the first day forward, I was overwhelmed with work: calling hotels, scheduling entertainment, and following up with guests. There were so many details, and few procedures were in place. I saw the opportunity to streamline functions through standardized checklists, but I was so busy putting out fires there was no time to be proactive.
>
> There was no time to enjoy Miami, either, even though I had just moved here to take the job. I needed to furnish my apartment, buy a car, and learn my way around town. Christy had no empathy for my situation. She was furious if I was a few minutes late, even when I worked 14-hour days! All she cared about was how I was handling every party detail.
>
> Christy micromanaged me, interrupting my work several times an hour to check up on me—and to push me harder. Every time I took on a new assignment, she would say, "We need to confirm whether these people will attend, and I need this done right away." Then, as always, she would remind me that I was there on probation and could easily be replaced.
>
> I finally realized that work was all she did . . . why would she think that people would want to go home before midnight?
>
> I decided I had to take a stand. The very next time Christy handed me a stack of paper at 4:45 PM, I said, "I'm so sorry, I won't be able to give this my best until tomorrow. I'll get to it first thing in the morning." Then, I picked up my keys and walked out with a friendly "Good night."
>
> Needless to say, Christy was fuming. But, the next day my job was still there. The smoke turned to a chill, but that was preferable to feeling like I only existed for Christy's business agenda.

Over the next week, I began to notice a change: Christy hadn't given me any work at the end of the day at all. Could it be that she was beginning to feel the tiniest bit of respect for my boundaries? Even if it was a tiny bit, it felt huge.

With demanding bosses, it really does require you to set your limits and communicate them clearly. Otherwise, the TOT who wants more, gets more. Sam risked alienating Christy forever by standing up to her. But had he not done so, Sam would have been trapped in Christy's world of escalating and unrealistic expectations.

TOT-Taming Tips: Demanding

Handling a demanding boss is a matter of great delicacy. You can't take it personally. You must approach the situation in a positive manner, disarming your TOT with a calm, professional, rational style—rather than getting swept up in the hysteria. Most importantly, keep your sense of humor.

Being even-keeled and having the ability to shake off stress is invaluable, especially with a ruthless manager. It's contagious. Here are some other gold mines—and mine fields—for dealing with the demanding:

 DON'T DO THIS ...

Support the Habit. Use your TOT as a role model and start every day off with a list that recaps her current orders—but while you're at it, add some of your own demands. Point fingers (and when needed, toes and elbows). Blame as many people as possible for the problems in the office. Recommend that your TOT invest in some listening devices and hidden cameras that monitor staff progress and hours 24/7. (Just make sure you're in charge of the project!)

Do This . . .

Set Expectations. When your boss gives you a new assignment, give her an estimate of how long it will take—and what you need to complete it. Since you have other jobs on your plate, this is a good time to let her know how the new request affects them. She may object to this reality check, but at least you're having the discussion beforehand, rather than after you've missed an impossible deadline. Create frequent and regular status reports so your boss understands that work is indeed in progress, before she even has to ask.

 DON'T DO THIS . . .

Be a Punching Bag. Take your lumps with a smile on your face—and cheerfully accept demand after demand. If your TOT blames you for something you didn't do, take "credit" anyway. "Actually, Sherrie forgot the invoices, but I would have done the same thing. I'm so hopeless!" Go ahead and assume responsibility for every other bad thing that happens: a bad lunch, the weather, or the stock market drop.

Do This ...

Speak the Truth. If your precautionary measures don't work, choose the right time and place, and let your boss know that you are feeling overwhelmed. Recap your current projects and their status. Make recommendations on projects that could be moved down the priority list or given to others. If you need more resources, you are going to have to enlighten your boss—and request them directly. Stay positive by accepting responsibility instead of pointing fingers. Say things like, "I feel that I won't be able to do a great job on X if I also have to complete Y by Wednesday," instead of, "Your plan to have Y done on Wednesday won't work."

 DON'T DO THIS ...

Buy a Gavel. When your TOT summons you to her office for a new project, treat it like a court case. Every time she issues an order, leap up and yell, "Objection!" When she objects to your constant objections, tell her that you are going to cite her for contempt unless she can give her summation. By the time she figures out the appeals process, you can be across town.

Do This ...

Be a Beacon of Reason. When you've successfully completed a project that your TOT foisted on you, tell him how you made it happen. Talk about how you set mutual, realistic goals with your colleagues and how you balanced your other priority commitments with those of the other people involved. Leverage your success to deliver a non-threatening message of how your boss can achieve greater results on future projects. And remember that levity can sometimes disarm a tense, demanding TOT.

 DON'T DO THIS . . .

Keep Score. Start carrying around a tally sheet and make a mark every time your boss makes another unreasonable demand. Post a scoreboard in the break room, and update it weekly, so the whole office knows the score. Take bets—and encourage other departments to list their TOTs' scores. You can even have playoff brackets at the end of the year.

Do This . . .

Reinforce Good Behavior. Reward your TOT with praise every chance you get, when he asks for something instead of demanding it. If possible, do it in front of his boss (Big TOT). Say things like: "It was so helpful when you explained why this project means so much to the company," or "I appreciated that you understood that we'd have to push back the Thompson project by a couple of days to tackle this new initiative," or "Thanks for your clear explanation about the project. I really understood why we had to push this project hard."

TOT-Busters Q&A

Question

Whenever my boss sees that I'm out of the office, she assumes I'm off doing something personal. She never checks my schedule to see that I'm actually at a meeting. If I'm gone for more than 20 minutes, she leaves a voicemail outlining three more projects on the horizon in a harsh tone. I feel like putting her in a time out. Any advice?

Answer

If you let your TOT interrupt every important task, she will quickly learn to exploit this, just like a toddler would. You need to clearly set boundaries. Let her know you are going to be busy by leaving a note on your chair—or sending a reminder e-mail. Make it clear that it's a work commitment (if it is)—and when you'll be back. If it's a personal commitment, you may want to also mention that your work is covered for the time you'll be gone. This is more proactive and should prevent that slew of emergency orders from above.

 Points to Remember

- Your demanding TOT is under a lot of pressure, even if it is self-inflicted. Some of those demands are being pushed to you.
- Critical comments shouldn't be taken personally, unless they are grounded in truth. If they are, address the root cause rather than fighting back with words.
- Set clear expectations and communicate regularly. Your TOT may not realize the hours—or resources—required to complete a task.

- Try to set mutually agreed-on goals—and clarify deadlines.
- Insecurity is at the root of many TOTs' demands. Increase your TOT's feeling of security by making your intentions clear.
- Reward your TOT's improved communications and project assignment methods with gratitude and praise.
- Stay positive—and keep your sense of humor.

4

Ignoring

About Ignoring

YOU'VE BEEN CHARGED with completing the annual needs assessment for your department and it's due to your boss at the end of this week. You collect information from all of your coworkers, you put everything together in a comprehensive document, and on Friday morning you place it on the desk of your Terrible Office Tyrant (TOT). And then ... nothing.

Friday passes without feedback. When you get in on Monday, it's the same story. Days go by, and you get nervous. You need your boss's approval because if she doesn't sign off within the week, none of the departmental requisitions can be approved.

You drop by her office. She's on the phone and avoids eye contact. You send an e-mail: "Did you have a chance to review the needs assessment document I sent you?" No response. You try your luck with your TOT's assistant, who tells you that the boss is tied up at home but "she probably has your report." Yikes!

Seven unreturned phone calls—and several fruitless trips to her office later—you begin to doubt yourself. You wonder why your TOT won't respond. Maybe it wasn't due until next Friday. Maybe you forgot to deliver it. Maybe you had a mental slip and included "Firing the boss" on the needs assessment. Then, miraculously, you see her in the hallway, two hours before the deadline.

She perks up when she sees you. "Great job," your TOT tells you. "I sent it on to the CEO without changing anything at all. Hey, can you start on the Phelps report? I'm absolutely buried here." She doesn't mention your tidal wave of messages, and you squander the split-second of glory you just received by wondering if she's checked her e-mail anytime in the last millennium.

But Why?

If you've ever experienced the great shut-out from a boss, you know how nerve-wracking such treatment can be. It's one thing to have a toddler cross his arms and refuse to acknowledge you because you've locked away the cookie jar. It's quite another to have a grown adult shun you for no discernible reason.

When a superior treats you like you have the plague, naturally, you first wonder if you're in hot water, and the longer the silent treatment lasts, the more you end up fearing an eventual pink slip. You only have so many tricks to coax a response from your distant TOT, so your anxiety grows.

Your elusive TOT isn't necessarily trying to wound you or make you fearful. The problem is that it's not easy to tell whether you are being consciously frozen out—or simply overlooked—because the behavior in both cases appears the same.

Yes, it's possible that he may be angry with you or be aware of some impending bad news, such as a layoff. But, it's also just as likely that he might simply be overwhelmed, distracted, self-absorbed, or oblivious.

In many cases, getting the brush-off from your boss is just like getting it from a small child, except that your boss can wield a bigger brush. Let's look at the similarities in behavior and the reason why it happens:

Ignoring Toddler Behavior	Ignoring TOT Behavior
Your toddler shoves a mound of raw blue clay in her mouth. "Spit it out," you command. She clamps her jaw, chews it, and shakes her head "No." You retrieve the glob, but then you get the silent treatment until cartoon time.	Your boss asks if you'd like to buy some of her daughter's school fund-raiser cookies. "No, thanks," you say. After that, she won't return your e-mails or calls.
After he finishes building his castle, you tell your child to put away the blocks because it's time for bed. He ignores you and grabs more blocks and keeps building. You ask, "Did you hear what I said?" He replies, "Yes."	You interview 189 candidates for the bookkeeper position and make your choice, but you need sign-off from your TOT. You e-mail, voicemail, and text him, to no avail. After three weeks, you ask if he's gotten any of your messages. He replies, "Yes."
Your toddler has been asked to bring some crayons to preschool. He ignores the note from his teacher, and when he finally gets it to you four days later, you have 30 minutes to dash out and buy the supplies.	Your boss has been asked to present the quarterly results to Super TOT, but ignored it. He brings the request to you several days later, saying, "I just found this e-mail from Peter. I need the presentation in the next half hour."
You've been calling for your child all over the house. You find that he has somehow opened the "child-proof mini-gate" in the family room and poured a large bottle of grape juice all over the carpet. He jumps up suddenly and yells, "Messy, Daddy. Clean it!"	It's late and you've looked everywhere for your boss. His office lights are out—but his car is outside. Suddenly, in the hallway, he bumps into you with a "Termination Notice" for two of your staff. He says, "This is messy. You'd better handle it," and walks off.

There are two major categories of TOT-related ignoring: harmless and naughty. Being ignored by a TOT is always irritating, but in most cases, inadvertent. When a toddler glued to her favorite DVD disregards repeated calls to dinner, you know she's just distracted. She'll snap out of it once you turn off the player.

Likewise, if your TOT wants to spend a few solitary hours in her office watching her awards acceptance video, and your communications are all ignored, she has nothing against you—she wants to break away. In this case, though, you can't hit the DVD "off" button and watch her snap out of it.

The Great Escape

TOTs often feel overwhelmed by the conflicting demands placed on them. One way to cope with the nonstop flood of people wanting her time is for her to duck out and disappear. So when she slinks away upon seeing you, it might not be because she thinks that you have cooties. Rather, she might just need to attend to her own project priorities or personal life.

Your TOT may also launch into brush-off mode when he wants to feel empowered. He fancies himself too important to spend too much time with any one subordinate. He loves the feeling of being so much in demand that he can't possibly squeeze you in—it makes him feel like a celebrity of sorts.

The Coldest Shoulder

Being ignored gets a little messier when there's a problem between you and your TOT. This could be a calculated move—but let's face it, it's easier on him than direct confrontation. He just leaves the scene, either physically or through communication channels. It could be that he's angry about your work performance, or about something you said, or an imagined slight. Regardless, you are left in the dark and do not have a chance to address your concerns.

These TOTs tend to lack good people skills, and so they practice avoidance. They are sometimes described as being passive-aggressive. They haven't developed the ability to confront uncomfortable situations and find it easier to just tune you out.

True TOT Tales

Catch Me If You Can

Sometimes, trying to get an answer from your boss can feel like trying to get a response from Santa. Ryan works at a graphic design firm on the West Coast, and spent much of his time tracking down Ellen, his elusive TOT:

> *Ellen is a one-way communicator. I don't know why she's like that—but she's always been that way. Maybe it's because she's overworked, or maybe she's just oblivious. All I know is that I can e-mail her until my fingers turn blue, and never see a response.*
>
> *It's not that Ellen completely avoids me. She comes to my office to chat almost every day about her own projects and personal life and I can't get a word in edgewise. If I try to spit out a single syllable about my projects, she gets up abruptly and, boom, she's gone.*
>
> *Last week, Ellen came around to talk, as usual. But I had a critical project, so I tried something new. Before I mentioned my pending report, I rolled my chair around my desk. I sat next to her with the document in hand, and, in effect, blocked my doorway. When I brought up the report, she tried to make her exit, but she was boxed in.*

*Believe me, it was a stretch for me to be so assertive, but I
had to talk to her. And so I asked my question and she
answered. She had no choice. The only reason it worked was
because she was stuck! I realized that I have to catch her
off-guard if I need her attention.*

*Since then, I've been more proactive. I get my materials
together more concisely and try to pose everything as "yes/no"
questions. But I have to be sneaky. I listen for her voice and
figure out the best spots to intercept her.*

*She still avoids me, but she says that I'm doing a good job. I
guess I'm going to have to continue to be crafty in getting my
five seconds of "quality time" with her.*

Ryan's ambush solution may not work over the long term, but
when Ellen was actively ignoring him, he needed to do something
different. More importantly, Ryan found a different tactic: to
capitalize on the five seconds he had with Ellen, he had to change
his approach.

First, he gave more consideration to the problem, and then
reframed his requests to allow a quick answer. Ryan demonstrated
to Ellen that he wasn't dumping his problems on her—he was
actually problem solving, and simply needed her confirmation.
Ryan's new technique demonstrated to Ellen that it was easier to
answer a well-considered question than to go out of her way to
ignore the query.

TOT-Taming Tips: Ignoring

If your boss vanishes every time you approach, or your e-mails and
voicemails go into an inexplicable abyss, it's time to try something
different. Here are some tips on getting the attention of your
elusive TOT—as well as things to avoid:

DON'T DO THIS ...

Tackle Your TOT. Don't let your boss escape your clutches even one more time. Study his patterns to learn the times he takes a break. Roll a huge potted plant a few feet from the break room door, and hide behind it. Wear camouflage and paint your face green. When he approaches, leap out, arms outstretched, and say, "Heyyy! Gotta question about these invoices." If he tries to push past you, just block the door and every attempt he makes to escape.

Do This ...

Schedule Regular Meetings. Urge your boss to meet with you regularly and explain the benefits from his perspective. Use examples of how it helped on a recent project. Suggest an agenda, frequency (such as once a week), and several possible time slots. Keep the meetings brief and on schedule. Regular meetings eliminate the need to constantly chase your boss down. But to ensure that the meetings actually happen, send a reminder a few hours ahead of time.

 DON'T DO THIS ...

Put Your Boss on "Ignore." When your ignores-you-'til-he-needs-you boss approaches, close your eyes, cover your ears tightly, and belt out the old childhood fallback, "La la la la, I can't hear you!" Try it out at the next all-company meeting. When your boss asks you for your progress report, wait until you have the attention of the entire team of Big- and Super TOTs. If you can, wait for a Board meeting. Then smile big and run through the routine. When everyone looks shocked, say, "Only joking. I really *can* hear. I learned that from my boss."

Do This . . .

Level with Your TOT. Sit down with your boss and express your concern and frustration about being ignored. Without pointing fingers, try to find out why she hasn't responded to you. You might discover that her behavior has nothing at all to do with you—she might be under enormous pressure or swamped with work. On the other hand, if she does have issues with your performance, ask for honest feedback so that you can remedy any problems. If she beats around the bush, ask her point-blank what *she* would do in your situation.

 DON'T DO THIS . . .

Sing a Sad, Sad Song. Let your boss know how devastated her cold behavior has left you. Deck yourself out in a spangled shirt, cowboy boots, and 10-gallon hat. Croon the saddest country song you know to the team—but rework the lyrics to be about your boss. As your colleagues and the management team gather round, point at your TOT, clutch your chest, fall to your knees, and wail, "I sent her e-mails, I sent her faxes. But the shut-out came like death and taxes!"

Do This ...

Repackage Your Ideas. Study your TOT's routines and find new ways to get his attention. Instead of sending long e-mails marked "urgent," package your messages and reports in a concise, lively format that is appealing to read. Leave enough white space and use bullets. Make your meetings and presentations visually interesting, interactive, and lively. If you can make his work more enjoyable in general, he'll respond to you more quickly.

 DON'T DO THIS ...

Consult a Psychic. When you can't figure out why your TOT ducks away from you at every opportunity, invite a mystic into your office. Show the mystic a photo of your boss, some unanswered e-mails that you sent, and a crisp $20 bill. If she finds no answer at first, ask her to summon your TOT's ancestors. You can request that your boss's beloved great-great aunt Lillian haunt your TOT until she finally agrees to meet with you. (This will probably cost you an extra $20.)

Do This ...

Do Some Detective Work. Try to put yourself in your TOT's shoes, and think about why your boss might need space from you. Ask your colleagues for clues. Have they been having trouble getting your TOT's attention? Do they know of any special issues affecting your boss's behavior? Are other priorities distracting her? You may learn she's overloaded and juggling too many projects to deal with you—or you may confirm that she's ignoring everyone because she hates talking to her team. If the latter is true, keep sleuthing ... through online job listings.

TOT-Busters Q&A

Question

I got hired two weeks ago, and my boss still hasn't met with me. I walked into her office on my first day to get instructions, but she just gave me a company handbook and told me to read it. A few days later, I went into her office again and she looked annoyed and handed me more reading material. I still have no job assignment. I'm getting worried that if I don't get something to do soon, I'll either be laid off, or bored to death here. What do you suggest?

Answer

You may have the world's most disorganized boss, but if you just can't get answers, take the bull by the horns. Figure out what project is the most mission-critical for the company and start offering your services to the project team. Send your boss a memo reporting your actions. "Given that I still have no formal assignment, I've decided to start working with the team on Project X." If that still results in no response—your job could be at risk. You might need to check with someone higher up the food chain to get the real story.

Points to Remember

- Being ignored is no fun, but try not to take it personally. Your boss might simply be busy or preoccupied.
- Find out why your boss has no time for you by asking directly and by asking your colleagues.
- If you've done something to irritate or disappoint your boss, try to communicate with your TOT in a nonthreatening, constructive way.
- Make it easy for your boss: set up regular meeting times, keep the meetings short, and make your reports or presentations appealing and creative.

5

Impulsiveness

About Impulsiveness

YOU AND YOUR TEAM are hatching a potentially lucrative new project: an air freshener code-named "Scentamint." The possibilities are tantalizing, but everyone on the team agrees—it's a project best kept under wraps until it's been fully explored. A premature revelation to senior management could derail the whole thing.

You pledge as a team to work together to collect the data, test the idea, and prepare it for a full presentation to the top brass—as soon as all the details have been worked out. You're working diligently on the project when your Terrible Office Tyrant (TOT) drops by with a surprise guest: the CEO of the company.

"I wanted to show the big guy what everyone's working on these days," your TOT blurts out. Luckily, you've just minimized the Project Scentamint logo on your screen in order to keep your project secret. You look to your manager and exchange what you think to be a knowing wink. You believe that your collective secret will hold . . . which is true, for about the next five seconds.

Your manager pauses and then begins to speak. "We're hatching a great new idea! It's really exciting. Have a seat. You're gonna love this one! Show him that awesome logo!" Within seconds, he blurts out the entire story and weeks of under-the-radar preparations for Scentamint have dissipated into thin air.

But Why?

What just happened? It's a classic case of impulsive TOT behavior. Toddlers will often pledge to behave, and then in a heartbeat, do the very thing they promised not to do. Although it seems unfair or shocking, an impulsive gesture is often not born from malice or forethought. It's simply the idea that popped into their heads at the moment, and so they followed through on it.

In toddlers, impulsiveness is a blurted secret, a snatched toy, or a dash into a busy street. In your TOT, it is a crazy out-of-the-blue project, a careless word to an employee or competitor, or a last-minute, time-consuming idea.

An impulsive TOT wreaks havoc on the office by shooting ideas, words, and orders out into the atmosphere with little or no regard for their impact. He is a walking, talking, knee-jerk reflex—no conscious thought, remorse, or understanding of the outcome.

Of all the TOT behaviors, impulsiveness can be the most disarming. The toddler who runs out into traffic to chase a ball gives no warning to his parents of his plan. He simply makes a dash for it, while horrified onlookers try to respond to the danger he's unleashed.

Similarly, a TOT is equally capable of uncorking impulsive behavior with no heads-up. You may be perfectly confident about your current course of action, and then your boss can parachute into your office with a hot new idea that sinks weeks of work right to the ground.

A Great Escape

Although impulsive behavior can seem reckless and thoughtless, it can also be exciting, free-spirited, and spontaneous.

Sometimes, these are positive qualities in a boss. After all, consider the antithesis—being stuck working for a boss whose core qualities are routine, tedium and inertia.

A boss willing to think outside the box can be a boss who takes the team to new heights of success and creativity. But at other times, he's the boss who interrupts your day with a never-ending stream-of-consciousness modus operandi.

How similar is the impulsive TOT to the impulsive toddler? Consider the parallels:

Impulsive Toddler Behavior	Impulsive TOT Behavior
She blurts out a family secret to the waiter at the new Italian restaurant downtown, "Mommy's not s'posed to drink wine. It makes her talk funny."	She blurts out news of a private nature during a team meeting: "Hey, Nancy, have you told everyone you're five months pregnant?"
He grabs a toy from a smaller child. "I see it. I want it. Now it's mine! And you can't have it."	He grabs a high-visibility account from a rival colleague. "Hey, this should have been ours, anyway. We've got the chops to pull it off . . . snooze, ya lose."
Your child nabs three boxes of that new sugary cereal from a grocery shelf and drops them into your overflowing cart. To make room, she tosses a loose bag of tangerines that roll out of control down aisle six.	Your TOT blows the equipment budget on a new 60″ plasma screen for the conference room. "Check it out. It's pricey, but so what?" Just then, every duct-taped-together computer in the office flames out, and the office goes dark.
She wants to put on a sock puppet show at midnight. "Wake up, mommy and daddy. We've got a very special show for you tonight!"	She wants to go for a two-hour lunch during your big deadline crunch. "I just realized I work you too hard. You can come back and finish afterward!"

What causes impulsiveness? It's the reflex to get what you want now, rather than wait and consider all options. In the old days, this was a pretty good policy. He who grabbed quickly ate more. He who took his time to think it over often found his lunch eaten by his buddy—or a pack of wolves.

Impulsiveness can also be an immature reaction to boredom. When there's not much going on to stimulate the brain, the curious mind may invent challenges for itself. In a toddler, that may mean dropping eggs from the counter to see what will happen, or smacking a sibling to see what he does in response. In an adult, these impulses may prompt taking a new risk or experimenting with a new way to tackle the same old grind.

No matter the cause, a manager who grasps for short-term glory or thrills, without consideration for the long-term impact, can be a menace.

The Impetus of Impulsiveness

If impulsive behavior can be harmful to a business, why do so many TOTs let their unpredictable sides rule the day?

Quick Decisions = Progress

Impulsive TOTs have been schooled to believe that a quick, decisive manager is the cream of the crop. This encourages some of them to act with little or no thought. When faced with any pause in the action, a TOT may fear that his lack of forward motion reflects badly on his reputation. He may make a "decisive" move simply for the perceived boost it will bring to his professional aura.

The Antidote to Overload

With far too much on their plates, managers often resort to impulsive behavior out of necessity. They simply can't handle the tsunami of demands placed on them. And so they make rash decisions out of an inability to make time for a more considered response.

Under the Radar

A TOT who acts impulsively with you may be trying to get out of the conversation as quickly as possible to keep his flaws under wraps. A long, complex discussion makes him sweat. He wants to give any answer—or skip the subject—just to move on. These managers are motivated by fear, and a speedy decision cuts down the amount of time you have to size them up.

Can't Be Bothered

A manager without regard for your project may act impulsively because she is apathetic. She's got bigger fish to fry. If your project isn't going to help her move up the food chain, she's not going to devote any time to it. You get whatever stray thought pops into her head at the moment.

True TOT Tales

Sudden Party Syndrome

Ted is a CPA at a major accounting firm. In his business, there is no time more stressful than tax season. Long hours are the norm and steady leadership is needed to keep the team on schedule and error-free. But Ted had the misfortune to work for a supervisor who handled the seasonal stress in his own special way. Here's his story:

> *At tax time, there's no one more focused than a CPA. We know we're facing a major deadline. Our work requires speed,*

precision, and attention to detail. A stray number or misplaced decimal point can spell disaster for us and our clients.

But my boss was incapable of handling the pressure that came with the crunch period. Throughout this stretch, he would routinely spring last-minute "stress-relief" parties on us.

Telling him no was not an option. Even though I barely saw my wife during tax season, I felt I had to humor my boss on these outings. Unfortunately, once we would comply with his whims, it triggered even more impulsiveness.

One night, my boss decided that sitting and drinking with us was not exciting enough, and so he began to dance on a nearby table. The regular patrons were delighted, but our team just shook our heads.

I decided to take serious steps to protect myself from this Sudden Party Syndrome. First, I paid careful attention to outside elements that seemed to trigger his impulsive behavior. For example, if his boss was coming down especially hard on him, I noticed that it often spurred him to vent. When his desk was finally clear of work, he'd want to celebrate and launch right into party mode.

So once I started to sense impending impulsivity, I would leave my office light on as a decoy and work down the hall in a rarely used conference room. When I heard the telltale signs of the boss rounding up unsuspecting colleagues for an insta-party, I would grab my laptop and sprint for the door, finishing my work at home.

The party finally came to a crashing halt: our boss slid off the table during one of his spontaneous dance routines and broke his ankle. This event was enough to get the attention of the senior partners, who wanted to know exactly why his entire CPA team was in a bar watching the boss spin and roll during tax season in the first place.

The top brass was appalled by the tales of Sudden Party Syndrome and shut the party animal down for good. We were never happier to get back to work!

Although Ted literally caught a lucky break, dealing with an impulsive boss can be a huge chore. Ted came up with a number of clever tactics for handling his TOT's impulsiveness:

- He stayed focused on the business tasks at hand and did not let his boss's behavior distract him.
- He learned to monitor for triggers.
- He planned a last-minute escape route.

TOT-Taming Tips: Impulsiveness

To manage a TOT with turbo-charged impulsive behavior, you need a host of strategies on hand. Some, as you might imagine, are more effective than others:

 DON'T DO THIS ...

Don't Look Back! When your boss impulsively changes direction on a project right before deadline, get on board with lightning speed. Throw out all of your previous work. Hold a bonfire in the parking lot or gather every shredder you can find. When anyone asks you what's going on, reply: "Can't talk now. Major change in strategic direction. Undo. Undo. Undo."

Do This ...

Tap the Brakes. Expect surprises and have a plan ready when your often-impulsive boss springs a surprise redirection on you. Review project changes with your TOT to confirm her new course. Show her what's been completed, what can be salvaged under her new vision—and what must be scrapped. This accomplishes two things: you'll give your boss time to think through her initial knee-jerk reaction, and you'll save yourself from the eventual back-tracking you'll have to face later to cover for your TOT.

 DON'T DO THIS ...

Set Yourself on Auto-Pilot to "Reject." Faced with another spur-of-the-moment new idea from your boss, automatically respond with "That's crazy!" Then follow up with a rant about how things always ran smoothly when the previous boss was in charge. Tell him that the idea conveys to upper management that the department is in chaos and the budget is being squandered. Finally, create an auto-reply to your boss's e-mails that reads: "Idea respectfully considered, and REJECTED."

Do This ...

Forecast the Outcomes. Rather than discarding new ideas outright, be specific about the possible impact of the impulsive behavior. If you know that specific negative outcomes will result if a plan moves forward, then list them, but remain factual, not confrontational. Help your TOT boss ponder the consequences.

DON'T DO THIS ...

Start a Revolution. Fed up with the unpredictability of life with a fickle boss? Present your boss with a list of demands from the staff and refuse to respond to any reasonable request for negotiation. Tell your boss: no predictability, no peace. Be sure to make a snazzy flag to carry on your frequent protest marches ... just leave the forwarding address for your last paycheck.

Do This ...

Build a Coalition. Instead of positioning your case as "you versus the boss," use "we" when trying to deflect an impulsive move. This projects the feeling that you and your TOT are in it together. By avoiding confrontation or putting forth the opposing viewpoint, a collaborative "team vision" will allow your TOT to see things more objectively.

 DON'T DO THIS ...

Let Your Guard Down. The moment things seem quiet around the farm, take the opportunity to relax. Put your feet up on your desk, swing open your door for air, and get some needed online shopping done for the new hamster wheel you've been thinking about. If the boss wants something done, it's likely you'll know about it soon enough.

Do This . . .

Stay One Step Ahead. TOT impulsiveness can sneak up on you, so be prepared at all times. Feeding new ideas to your boss on a regular basis is not only good for career advancement, it also helps prevent impulsive bosses from giving you last minute projects to light a fire under you! Always have a stockpile ready of new initiatives and demonstrate that you are proactive. If you want to get ahead, be thinking of future possibilities so your boss doesn't have to go overboard on your behalf.

TOT-Busters Q&A

Question

Several times a week, my boss calls me into her office to share her latest brainstorm. Often, her ideas are just totally off the wall—unachievable, unaffordable, just pie in the sky kind of stuff. These meetings are torture. She tells me to drop everything else she's assigned me and tackle her new big idea. So I follow her orders and move into high gear and sure enough, three days later, she puts the new project on hold—or just kills it. I suspect her ideas are being shot down by higher ups because they don't make any sense. But I'm stuck in the middle, running around in circles. What should I do?

Answer

Your TOT is setting this breakneck pace for her ideas and you're letting yourself get sucked in, at least until someone more senior has the sense to put on the brakes. By acting collaboratively when she unveils her next impulsive brainstorm, you might be able to break out of this loop. Diplomatically ask questions that help her see the ramifications of her latest big idea. Inquire how this project fits into the company's strategy, or what kind of profits it will generate. If you can help her focus on the big picture, you will, at worst, have more clarity on how to proceed. At best, she may even scrap the idea before you leave her office.

 Points to Remember

- Slow the pace down by asking questions and sharing information. Your curiosity will help you understand your boss's motives—and send a signal to your boss that you will typically need more information before proceeding with an impulsive idea.
- Know the triggers to your TOT's impulsiveness. Being prepared for it makes it easier to handle.
- Don't argue when faced with another impulsive directive, but do have a strong justification ready for staying the course. When you need to stand your ground, be calm and professional.
- Help your TOT understand the impact of an impulsive decision. Help her weigh the alternatives, and show her the cost of changing direction.
- Fill the idea vacuum yourself. If your TOT loves new ideas, rise to the occasion and contribute your own.

6

Lying

About Lying

IT'S A GORGEOUS DAY outside. Sunny, blue skies, 75 degrees—in other words, perfect. But, lo and behold, here comes your Terrible Office Tyrant (TOT) shuffling down the hallway, sniffling and coughing.

"Wow," he says, "I guess winter's not over yet because I think I've got the flu. I gotta get home and eat some chicken soup and crackers."

You nod sympathetically and tell him to take care of himself. But as you fuss with the windows to get some of that fresh air, you see a much more sprightly version of your TOT skipping to his car. And, eureka, he throws his briefcase into the trunk, pulls out golf clubs and throws them into his buddy's waiting SUV.

Almost every kid has tried faking illness to get out of school. Unfortunately, there's always a mom or dad who sees through that brilliant scheme—and it's off to school once again.

Unless you were the most saintly of children, you can now recognize the signs of faux illness, so when your boss starts moaning and groaning on every sunny day, you smell a rat. You can't yell "Liar, liar, pants on fire," if you want to keep your job, and so you bite your tongue and try to ignore your gnawing aggravation.

But Why?

Brace yourself . . . sometimes, bosses lie. Okay, with that shocking news out of the way, let's delve into why they lie and what you can do about it.

There are two main types of lies told by TOTs: those that cause damage and those that don't. Most office deception falls into the white-lie category. For instance, Golfing TOT wants to impress everyone with his dedication. But even though he does stay late and cranks out reports quickly, he still feels the need to feign illness to take off a half-day out of a 60-hour week.

Or, you may have a boss who hammers away at her computer keyboard looking terribly overworked, but her monitor is sometimes turned away so that you won't see she's viewing "Great Destinations" web sites.

Sometimes those minor TOT deceptions can actually save you some grief because, face it, you'd rather not have your boss say that you looked like an elf in your new green suit. On the other hand, big lies mean big trouble. Some TOTs will lie to their clients about delivery dates and then expect you to drop everything to meet the impossible schedule. "You don't want the client to think I'm a fibber!" says the TOT-in-denial. (Check out Chapter 13 on *Fantasy World* to learn more about bosses living in La-La Land.)

Others will assign blame to their staff for botched work or missed deadlines (with the misguided belief that constant lying is preferable to occasional, human mistakes). If your TOT routinely tells big lies that get people into trouble, endanger your reputation, or border on unethical—then the scope of TOT taming has been exceeded. It's time to set your e-mail for Out-of-Office Auto Reply . . . permanently.

The lies told by kids and TOTs are often prompted by similar triggers, but, of course, when your boss toys with the truth, it can affect your livelihood. Let's take a look:

Lying Toddler Behavior	Lying TOT Behavior
Your toddler decides to bake a cake all by himself. He mashes a chocolate bar into a slab of butter and gets it all over the house. When you confront him, he says, "Doggie did it, not me."	Your boss decides to redo your presentation slides, replacing graphics with headache-inducing charts. His boss, the CEO, throws a fit and your TOT claims, "Yeah, the team went wild on these slides."
You overhear him telling kiddies, "Me going to meet Super Mouse and stay in his Mouse House. We best friends," right before your annual trip to Superworld Park.	You overhear him tell his colleagues, "I'll be going to the Leadership Vision Symposium next week," although he just told you he's getting laser eye surgery at the Leadership Vision Clinic.
After she creates a mess of doll paraphernalia around her room, your toddler comes out to watch television. When you ask if she cleaned up her room, she says, "Yes," and looks away.	You give him your cash flow analysis for review, but it just sits on his desk. When you ask on day 11 if he's read it yet, he says, "Uh huh," and then quickly changes the subject.
He plays "king of the world" with his best friend, who is appointed the obedient subject. When his friend tries to grab the crown, he says, "You'll be king next time." But next time, he tells his friend, "No, I'm king. You be king next time."	When your TOT hires you, he promises you that "you'll be promoted in six months." After six months, you ask about your promotion. He says, "You'll get it for sure if you prove yourself by your one-year anniversary."

Pinocchio stopped lying so he could be a real boy, whereas TOTs often lie because they want to be perceived as real authority figures. An ethical boss will confess when he errs and will attempt to learn from his mistakes. A less ethical boss will duck out the door and pretend to know nothing about the issue. A very unethical boss will point the finger at you, or at his team.

The Lure of the Lie

Your boss probably wants to climb the corporate ladder, and in the cutthroat scramble to gain prestige and the attention of a Big- or Super TOT, he may overstate his accomplishments or hide his mistakes. He's so desperate to ascend up the chain, that he might actually convince himself that his white lies are true. What starts out as fibbing to others turns into self-deception, which can become so entrenched that your TOT loses touch with the truth.

Your boss also might lie if he fears getting nailed for something he did—or didn't do. Like kids who deny getting chewing gum embedded in the new carpet because they fear the Mom's wrath, TOTs often deny their role in a project's failure, in miscalculating problems, or in anything that goes wrong. Simply put, your boss doesn't want to get fired any more than you do.

Finally, TOTs sometimes lie because they think it's nobler to tell a little white lie than to speak the unfettered truth. Your boss may want to shelter you from criticism, so she doesn't tell you when a customer complains about you. She may think you'll improve your performance in time, so she refrains from pointing out your mistakes, even when you ask for feedback. Or, she might simply want to avoid dealing with any emotional fallout from putting forth the facts.

True TOT Tales

Spinning the Spin-Off

Sarah worked in operations at the headquarters of a regional real estate brokerage company. When she was unexpectedly offered a new job opportunity, her TOT ended up lying to her in order to keep her on board. Here's Sarah's story:

My boss, Peter, headed the firm's new commercial real estate division. Revenues climbed substantially over a period of two years, and soon Peter told me that our division might spin off from the parent company with him at the helm. "Keep it confidential," he said, assuring me if the deal happened, I would become a senior manager.

Not long after, I had another offer come to me through a recruiter. I felt that I had to let Peter know because I was seriously considering a change. He didn't want me to jump ship, so he exaggerated the benefits I would reap if I stayed. He said I'd have a lot more authority, money, and ownership in the company.

He convinced me that the spin-off was a done deal, so I opted to stay. But whenever I asked when the transition would happen, Peter would say, "I think it's imminent." I started to hate that word.

About three months later, I had lunch with our executive vice president, David. He mentioned that there was going to be a 30 percent cut in our division. "I thought you knew," he said. Peter was at the table, and I saw his face turn red from embarrassment.

Afterward, I asked Peter when he had discovered the division was scaling down. He said, "Well, you know about these things. One minute business can retract and the next, you're gold." I realized then that the layoffs had been discussed for a couple of months and Peter chose not to disclose that to me.

I don't think that Peter's motives were malicious, but his deception caused me to decline a good job opportunity. I'm still unclear if his actions resulted from wishful thinking, or if he knowingly conveyed false information to string me along.

I did learn a valuable lesson working with Peter; whenever something sounds too good to be true, it probably is. Now

I know that it's essential to do my homework, talk to people, and ask questions, so that a manager can't pull the wool over my eyes.

Sarah learned the hard way that you can't believe everything your bosses tell you. This is a tough situation because you need to be able to trust them (as well as your colleagues). However, when your own well being and future is on the line, it pays to ask questions. Because trust is a two-way street, you can't push back too aggressively if you don't believe what your TOT has told you, but you do have the right to be curious.

Remember to give your boss an opportunity to gracefully back out of a false statement. If you corner your TOT, he may create new lies to cover old ones—or worse, lash out at you.

TOT-Taming Tips: Lying

Hopefully, you'll never be in a situation where your TOT tells you that "you can't handle the truth." After all, the untruths are harder to handle. With a wide variety ranging from little fabrications to bold-faced lies, you need tools to deal with frequent fibbers. Here are some TOT Taming Tips that will help you out:

 DON'T DO THIS ...

Say, "Your Nose Is Growing Longer." When your boss tells you that he was at the top of his class at MIT, laugh and slap your knees. Say, "Boss, your nose is so long, it just bumped me in the forehead." Tell him you know that he actually attended the Mixologist Institute of Tacoma, where he was voted World's Worst Bartender.

Do This ...

Get to the Bottom of the Lie. Try to discover what motivates your boss to lie. Discover the details of the situation before jumping to conclusions. For instance, suppose your boss made a huge mistake, miscalculating a revenue forecast. You know that when his own TOT, Big TOT, asked how the account was going, he didn't reveal his error. On investigation, you find out he lied with the intention of fixing the mistake before the Big TOT ever found out. In short, don't judge until you have all the facts.

 DON'T DO THIS ...

Weave Your Own Tangled Web. Practice for your ascendance to TOThood by inflating your own accomplishments—and invent the truth. When your boss asks how you're progressing on the Chapman account, puff out your chest and say, "Great. I've just about got it wrapped." Since you didn't even know you were supposed to be working on it, grab any Chapman paperwork you can find and smear it across your desk. Invite your boss in and show her the multiple files. Smile and put your hands in the "raise the roof" position when you tell her, "And, here it is."

Do This ...

Be a Good Role Model. Always be honest with your boss, and indicate that you would like the same respect. Admit to mistakes early. Tell her that you've learned that the truth, although sometimes painful, is the right thing. Don't expect quick results or even a retraction of old lies, but setting a good example will help her better deal with tough issues in the future.

 DON'T DO THIS ...

Lead the Crusade for Truth. The next time your boss tells you he has to work on an important client e-mail, and you know perfectly well that he's actually watching all the latest YouTube videos on his computer, barge into his office with a megaphone and shout, "Hey everyone, bring in the popcorn. Matinee is on!"

Do This ...

Don't Play Dumb. If your boss tells a lie, you might be tempted to just ignore it because you don't want to deal with the confrontation. Hammering your boss with accusations won't work, but you can't let dishonesty continue forever. If your boss tells a lie, pose some gently probing questions. By asking her to recap and elaborate, it will be harder for her to fabricate. If the versions don't match up, you can say "I'm confused, boss. Was it (x), as you said before, or (y) as you're saying now?" Allow your boss an opportunity to "clarify" her position and save face. Try to inspire her to live up to your expectations of integrity.

DON'T DO THIS ...

Bring in a Palm Reader. Tell your TOT you know he lied, so you've asked your personal palm reader to come in and tell him of his dark future. Consider staging this confrontation in a public gathering, such as at the annual awards banquet, so that your boss will have the prestige of a large audience. *Caution:* He may continue to lie, and tell you how much he likes palm readers.

Do This ...

Mind Your Own Shop First. Remember, "Those who live in glass houses . . ." Have you ever stretched the truth or asked someone to cover for you during a long lunch? Don't get righteous about integrity issues if you don't follow the straight and narrow. Instead, pave the way for better communication by not reacting to lies in a temperamental tone. Try to discover his motivation, and exercise compassion and patience.

TOT-Busters Q&A

Question

My boss gives me assignments with false deadlines, which becomes apparent later. Recently, she told me one assignment was due in two days. I know for a fact that the report isn't actually due for another two weeks. She's just pushing me because she doesn't trust me to get the work in on time. Should I generally call her bluff, or just bite the bullet and stay up all night to get projects done?

Answer

Here's a case where it makes sense to question your boss for details. Ask her politely why the deadline is so tight. Tell her that the quality of the project would be much better if you had additional time. If you feel it's safe ground, and this has become a blatant practice, ask her diplomatically if there is a trust issue. If you're doing everything humanly possible and the result is mediocre reports, you're no worse off anyway. Try to negotiate a compromise, such as offering to get it to her by the week's end, and then casually tell her that you'd love it if she would establish deadlines with you based on your ability to submit your best work.

 Points to Remember

- TOTs often lie out of fear of looking bad or getting in trouble.
- TOTs may lie to inflate their image.
- Undermining your TOT's image by intimating he's a liar will always backfire.
- Get the entire story before jumping to conclusions about your TOT's integrity.
- Clean your own house before worrying about your boss's honesty level.
- Save face and show compassion rather than judgmental behavior.
- Try to encourage your boss to reveal the facts and live up to your expectations.
- If your TOT's lies cause people harm, you need to find a new job.

7

Self-Centeredness

About Self-Centeredness

YOU'VE SPENT A MONTH trying to salvage the Pawlife Dog-Mint Chews account due to the client's cutbacks, and now it's time to give a preliminary internal presentation to your agency management. All eyes turn to you, so you begin to talk about how you'll persuade the mega client to stay with your firm for their big launch. Three sentences later, your Terrible Office Tyrant (TOT) interrupts:

> "I suggested the yellow background on the presentation cover. It looks sharp, don't you think? Let me tell you how I got the Pawlife account in the first place, because it wasn't a picnic."

You don't get another word in for the entire meeting. Your boss takes all the questions from the staff, gives all the answers, and acts as if she alone discovered the heartbreak of bad canine breath. So who gets invited to the VIP kick-off dinner? One hint . . . not you.

But Why?

Sometimes TOTs behave as if they exist in a universe created solely for their own gratification. Like the toddlers who won't let anyone else near their stuff, the self-absorbed TOT won't let anyone else near whatever kudos or fun the workplace might yield. It's not that your TOT purposely wants to sabotage you or deny you satisfaction at work; it's that she wants it all for herself. With a self-centered TOT, your needs don't even enter into the picture.

This kind of TOT rarely engages in anything that doesn't result in immediate benefit to herself. If she assigns you a challenging new project and you succeed, she'll find a way to make it look like her brilliant idea. If she enters your cubicle with a question, it probably has to do with something she wants for herself. And if by some miracle she invites you out to lunch, the conversation will go something like this:

TOT   "I've got to work at least 60 hours this week if there's any hope of me winning that Division Three Award in November. I need to wrap this thing up so I can get to my condo in St. Barts in December. I think I'll spend the month there. I need a break."

You   "I know what you mean. I put in 90 hours last week myself and ..."

TOT   [cutting you off]: "So do you think you can come into work on Sunday to get this thing out the door for me? I have tickets to the opera, so I won't be there."

Office life requires some degree of cooperation, but the self-centered boss does not play well with others. Instead of drawing on the strengths of each team member, she suppresses everyone else so that she can shine and get her own needs met. In fact, some egotistical TOTs get so caught up in their own agendas that they can be oblivious to the needs of Big TOT or even Super TOT and can end up sabotaging themselves.

Let's take a closer look at how the world seems to revolve around self-centered toddlers and TOTs:

Self-Centered Toddler Behavior	Self-Centered TOT Behavior
Your toddler holds her stuffed turtle to her chest and screams, "Mine!!!" when you try to touch it.	Your TOT moves the coffee maker from the break room into his office, and tells you to run across the street to get your own, and bring him a biscotti while you're at it.
She demands more mashed potatoes and when you say, "No, those potatoes are for Aunt Judy," she grabs a handful off of Aunt Judy's plate and stuffs them in her face.	She grabs a custard croissant from your desk. When you say, "Actually, they're for the staff meeting later," she takes one anyway. "I'll just take yours. I'm hungry."
He barges into the room and insists that you watch him on his tricycle. When you tell him, "Not now, later," he screams, grabs you by the arm, and demands that you watch him "now!"	He barges into your cubicle as you meet with a client and insists that you review a document for him immediately. The document turns out to be his lunch order.
Your child rips the wrapping paper off of her present from cousin Tyler, throws her new doll across the room, and refuses to say thank you when prompted by you.	Your boss grabs the proposal that you stayed up all night to prepare, throws it on her desk without looking at it, and instead of thanking you, asks when your status report will be done.

Like bad bosses depicted in memorable films and TV shows, the typical TOT focuses so much on becoming (or remaining) numero uno, that she simply has no room in her world for you. Egocentric TOTs allow their employees no personal life or margin for error—and make their staff drop everything to serve their tiniest whims.

Climbing the corporate ladder takes intensity, ambition, and sometimes, ruthlessness. On the way up, you have to fight off competitors and constantly prove your worth. It's an energy-consuming endeavor, particularly in a time of rampant lay-offs, so the TOT might have little energy left over for think-ing about anything other than how to maintain his or her position.

A TOT without positive self-esteem is constantly on the alert for threats that might dethrone him, and so you'd bet-ter stay out of the way. Plus, the TOT has to rule his king-dom, which, for the barely competent, poses an overwhelming challenge. If you interrupt his efforts by having any needs at all, the TOT becomes colicky, impatient, and sometimes out of control.

Corporate culture often encourages self-centered behavior. Employees who don't stand up for themselves get trampled in many offices. And since egos can grow on the way to the top if not kept in check, many in the ranks fashion themselves after such role models.

Self-centered behavior is normal and even healthy among toddlers, who are still developing their identity. They need to focus on themselves until they get a solid sense of who they are. To some degree, it's also normal for TOTs to be self-centered, especially new managers who don't yet feel secure in their posi-tions. The problems occur when the TOT is so wrapped up in his own desires that he uses you as a doormat as he sprints toward his personal goals.

True TOT Tales

The Boss Who Won My Award

Layla worked as a project manager for a learning management company. Ironically, she acquired an unpleasant "learning" of her own about self-absorbed managers. Here's Layla's story:

> A few years ago, we were tasked with developing an e-learning program to help medical personnel understand new safety procedures. I headed a team of 12 designers, writers, and software developers.
>
> We worked very well together, and in record time, we developed an innovative program that integrated video, audio, and interactive tools. The client company liked the product so much that they submitted it to a national review board and we won a prestigious multimedia award for our efforts.
>
> When the award plaque arrived, we were so proud. My team debated about where to hang it. The lunchroom? The hallway? The main lobby?
>
> Our deliberations turned out to be for naught because my boss came by and saw us talking.
>
> "What are you doing congregating on work time?" he asked me.
>
> When I explained that the plaque had just arrived, he swooped down, grabbed the award out of the box, and told me to end the work disruption immediately by sending everyone back to their desks.
>
> The next day, the plaque hung on my boss's wall next to his framed bachelor's degree. He hadn't participated in the project at all, but he claimed the award as his own. I was incredibly disappointed, but as the team leader, I felt that I owed my team some reward. We went out for a nice dinner—and made sure we celebrated on our own.

Layla's boss was a particularly self-centered boss, and as she learned, it's not easy to handle this variety of TOT. Her response to the plaque pilfering was very selfless, and was probably the best approach. By taking the team out to dinner (instead of using company time), she was able to free herself and her colleagues from the strong gravitational pull of her boss's self-centeredness.

TOT-Taming Tips: Self-Centeredness

Remember that in the development process, it's natural for babies to think only of themselves for a time, until they grow in awareness. Similarly, TOTs must learn that their selfish actions have consequences for other people, that they'll win no friends by ignoring others, and ultimately, that their egotism can boomerang.

You can't do much to accelerate this maturity progression. For a self-consumed TOT, nothing you can do will ever be enough. Some TOTs can be so oblivious to the needs of others that they're almost impossible to be around. If your boss is so egotistical or rude that it affects the quality of your work, or immense stress, start looking for a new position, pronto. On the other hand, if your TOT is self-centered within tolerable bounds, and you can accept it, then these tips will help you to survive.

 DON'T DO THIS . . .

Enter the Land of Me-Me. When you're in the middle of impressing your colleagues with the story about how you repaired the copy machine by removing a dead mouse from the inside, don't let your boss ruin it by interrupting with his own epic vermin story: The Rat in the Hat. Hog the spotlight or your TOT will surely steal it from you. As soon as your boss starts to interrupt, yell "Excuse me!" at the top of your lungs, and swing your toner-covered mouse by the tail until you have everyone's attention; then continue your story. You can bet your TOT won't have his rat handy.

Do This ...

Cooperate. Help your boss learn how to work well with others by giving others credit and letting them shine in front of your boss. While it may take him a while to notice, he'll eventually realize that you don't crave the spotlight as he does, and it may give him pause. It also helps to expose him to other TOTs who neither desire constant attention nor appreciate his thirst for it. Mention how popular the CFO is among the staff because of her self-effacing style. If your company offers employee awards, let your TOT know about all the CFO's nominations. (Of course, you may want to reread the chapter on *Territorialism* first.)

 DON'T DO THIS ...

Give Your TOT a Lesson in Scale. Tired of your boss constantly acting like the world revolves around her? Casually walk into her office carrying a three-foot globe and say, "Boss, I'd like to play a game called 'Where in the world?' with you." Pull out a big pin and stick it squarely at the location of your office. Then say, "This pin represents our company. Notice that we cover less than one-billionth of the surface of this globe? There are 6.7 billion other people living on the planet, so that doesn't exactly make either of us the Center of the Universe."

Do This . . .

Help Your TOT See the 360° View. If your TOT takes any small step in refocusing toward you or others, praise her lavishly. When she does something that has negative consequences for you or the team, point out the effect of her actions.

 DON'T DO THIS . . .

Bang a Gong. If your boss routinely traps you at meetings for hours so that he can pontificate about his latest projects, pull out a mallet and start hitting a gong. Bang it with all your might until he covers his ears, and then say, "Boss, I'll be using this new time management tool. And . . . time-is-up."

Do This . . .

Help Your TOT Plan Ahead. If you know that your TOT gets carried away talking about herself or demanding that her needs get met after-hours, start giving her advance notice. "Boss, I'm leaving tomorrow at five because I have a personal appointment I can't miss." When tomorrow comes, remind her first thing in the morning that you'll be leaving on time. At 4:30 PM, tell her that you only have 30 minutes left, so if there's anything she needs she should tell you right away. Eventually, she'll get the idea that you also have needs and schedules that you must meet.

TOT-Busters Q&A

Question

I always keep a jar of candy on my desk for customers and staff. Last week, I brought in some pricey chocolates. My boss said, "Ooooh, I love these. I need them," and she took the jar to her desk. I fumed until she left, then went into her office and took the jar back. She didn't say anything later because the jar was empty, but now I won't refill it for fear of her grabbing it again. What do you suggest?

Answer

Buy your boss her own jar of candy. When you give it to her, say, "The candy on my desk is for my team to share—they really like it. I thought you might like a jar of your own, which you can refill." But remember to keep your jar stocked for when you need to lure her to your office for five minutes of her time.

 Points to Remember

- When self-centered bosses feel secure, they become less egocentric.

- Praise any unselfish behavior demonstrated by your TOT. Ironically, that ego stroke will encourage selflessness.
- Model good teamwork to show that no one person can carry the entire office.
- Find ways to make your needs known that enlighten—instead of provoke—your boss.
- Help your boss understand the effects of selfish actions.

8

Stubbornness

About Stubbornness

YOUR TERRIBLE OFFICE TYRANT (TOT) asks you to organize the fall conference. Your goal is to increase attendance by 100 percent, so you outline a brilliant marketing campaign and present your ideas to him, expecting great praise and celebration.

"You can't use this conference logo," he says, grimacing at your materials. "You should use the logo from last year."

"But last year you said never to use that logo again," you venture. "Is there a particular reason why we're using last year's logo again?"

"I decided I want to use last year's logo. It worked fine."

You move on to your next agenda item. "We can run an ad on that online small business site. It's very affordable."

"No, I don't think so," he says.

"But that's a top site for our target customer."

"No," he repeats, cutting you off. "We can't do that. You're giving the Internet too much weight. The answer is no." And so it continues with every one of your ideas, until you end up with a campaign exactly like last year's.

But Why?

A stubborn TOT treats change as if it has cooties—unless she initiates the change. Her bull-headed approach makes it nearly impossible for you to do your job well because you encounter resistance at every turn. When you try to improve things or get creative, the TOT toughens, and opts for the familiar rut. If you prove her wrong, she looks for a way to prove herself right and, of course, to have the last word.

She justifies her immobility in many ways. A favorite is to blame the bureaucracy. She says, "We can't try this new idea . . . upper management won't approve." Then she tells you that she's protecting you from humiliation because, as a company veteran and overall expert, she knows the ropes. "Without me," she says, "you'd hang yourself."

Unfortunately, in saving you from humiliation, your TOT constantly scrutinizes your innovative ideas for weaknesses—instead of thinking about the benefits. She doesn't necessarily want to make you feel incompetent: she simply fears stretching outside of her comfort zone and looks for an excuse to remain planted just where she is.

If she can't find anything wrong with your suggestion, she resorts to the tried-and-true tactic of saying "No" without any justification at all, like a three-year-old who refuses to put away her stuffed giraffe simply because she doesn't want to.

Toddlers and TOTs share many similar stubborn traits. Here are a few of the most common:

Stubborn Toddler Behavior	Stubborn TOT Behavior
Your toddler refuses to go to bed even when her head rolls to the side, her puzzle piece falls out of her hands, and drool rolls down her chin.	Your TOT refuses to end a late meeting, even after the staff begins yawning and tapping, the janitors turn off hallway lights, and your boss begins nodding off himself.
He refuses to play with cousin Jimmy. When you ask if he wants to play blocks with his cousin, he screams, "No!" When you hand Jimmy the blocks, your child grabs them back, howling, "No, my blocks!"	The boss refuses to let the new intern sort through the mound of folders spilling into the hallway. "Boss," you say, "We're desperate. Lisa can clear this backlog." "I'm sure you can handle it yourself," she says. "Lisa doesn't have the can-do attitude my project needs."
Your toddler yanks the heads, arms, and legs off all of her dolls, and throws the various parts all over the room. "Help me pick up the dollies," you demand, starting to collect them yourself because you have visitors coming. "No, no, no," she yells, hurling herself on top of the Dead Doll Graveyard.	Your TOT refuses to streamline her mega-memo about break room clean-up policies. "Boss," you say, "nobody will read all this." She retorts, "When will you learn that details are important?" Her 60mb memo with diagrams freezes her e-mail, so she prints out 100 copies.
She tries to stick the hippo puzzle piece into the guppy-shaped hole 20,000 times, and gets angry when you offer the correct piece. She angrily rejects your suggestion and goes back to pounding Harry Hippo into Gary Guppy's tail.	Your boss uses the same ineffective sales pitch 20,000 times and gets angry when you suggest that she try something new. "This exact pitch built this company," she hisses.

When toddlers get the "No, No" bug, we call it the "Terrible Twos" and hold our breath until they outgrow it. Child-rearing experts say that toddlers refuse to do what you want because they need a way to differentiate themselves from you, establish independence, and test the limits of their power. They say that this willful behavior is, in fact, healthy.

The Roots of Stubbornness

TOTs, on the other hand, have no need to figure out how much power they can wield by digging in their heels. When they display obstinate behavior, it's usually because they're fearful. They worry that if they change course or try something new, things will go awry. Taking the unknown path could lead them to great losses: losing face, money, the executive parking spot, the love of Big TOT, or even losing their job.

Another reason that TOTs become so entrenched in their way of doing things is that they get the idea that being boss means acting firm to the point of pig-headedness. The stubborn TOT believes that strong leaders don't "cave," and so he won't relent even when he's obviously, embarrassingly, wrong.

Your TOT's inflexible behavior may also be linked to laziness. If the change you propose entails one iota of more work for him, he wants nothing to do with it. Even thinking about change can tax a TOT, and so he struggles to conserve his mental resources by just saying "No!" before he thinks through your proposition.

- -

True TOT Tales

Stubborn Awakening

Jenny was a paralegal who worked for a TOT whose ways were carved in stone. Jenny's enthusiasm for new projects upset the apple cart almost as much as if she wasn't doing any work at all. Here's Jenny's story.

Within a couple of months of starting my job, I became so good at it that I usually finished all my work in half a day. By noon, I had nothing left to do. So I volunteered to take on additional duties.

However, my boss told me there was nothing extra for me to do. I mentioned that another department might have work for me. She said that company policy wouldn't allow me to work in two departments.

Finally, I said that she could cut my job to half time and save the department money. Instead of being happy about my proposal, she nearly fired me on the spot. She said something about being "unwilling to lose a full-time allocated slot" and that I had been hired to work full-time, and not to slack off.

After that, she nitpicked my work to death. She tried to fill up my time by making me redo everything. She just couldn't adjust her "full-time allocation" mindset, even if it would yield better results. As a result, my motivation was sapped.

A couple weeks later, she came to my office and ranted that I had taken a three-hour lunch. I didn't argue, since making myself scarce was one of my solutions to the situation, but I told her I was caught up on my work. "Then, find something else to do," she screamed. I said, "Well . . . what do you suggest?"

To my surprise, that open-ended question was what finally worked. "Why don't you take on the Corestell project?" she asked. "I'm working 80 hours a week and you're dining out! I need to get that thing off my plate."

So I learned that when the ideas came from her, she could be flexible. From that point forward, whenever I had a suggestion, I'd always find a way to put the ball in her court so that she felt as if she had come up with it herself. Otherwise, she wouldn't budge once her mind was made up.

Jenny was caught between a rock and a hard place. Her stubborn boss didn't appreciate Jenny's initiative in trying to take on new responsibilities, and Jenny's ensuing boredom and new tedious assignments caused her to lose interest in her job and leave the scene for a little too long. Fortunately, instead of getting fired, Jenny finally broke through to her boss—and both are much happier.

Jenny stumbled on the best system to relieve her restlessness—by politely putting the onus on her boss.

TOT-Taming Tips: Stubbornness

The boss who won't change his mind, no matter how ridiculous his position, can be a recurring nightmare. The more aggravated he makes you, the more inclined you might be to argue with him to try to make him see reason. And the more you argue, the more stubborn he gets, so the cycle of resistance builds on itself until you're locked into a power struggle that you invariably lose.

You don't have to lock horns with your bull-headed boss. Instead, practice these TOT-taming tips.

 DON'T DO THIS . . .

Blast Him into Agreeing. Steal the subwoofers out of your kid's low-rider, bring them to your office, and hide them under a pile of annual reports. Blast your favorite death-metal or rap track, then freestyle your project update in rhyming verse. When your boss yells, "Where is that noise coming from?" continue blaring: "My project's done, so I'm on the run. If you say no, you'll see a real show!" All the chaos will have the desired effect. In exactly 39 seconds, he'll sign anything you hand him.

Do This . . .

Choose Your Words. Use positive language to relax your boss when he's stuck in a stubborn rut. Always begin with some sort of affirmation: "Thanks for doing such a great job of preparing me for that meeting." When it comes time to make your request, convert your closed-ended question into something more open-ended. So instead of asking if you can leave early, which always seems to invite a no response, say "I've finished working on the Pratt report and got in really early. Thanks for all your guidance on it. It would be so helpful if I could leave a bit early—my eyes are a little crossed. How does 4:30 PM sound?"

 DON'T DO THIS . . .

Turn on the Tears. Chop an onion on your desk, and when your eyes turn red and puffy, head straight into your boss's office. Shuffle your feet as you enter, look down, and then slump into a nearby chair. Say, "Boss, I'm so depressed. It's my frog, Freddy. Gone. I was so despondent, I could barely drag myself to work this morning, but then I thought that maybe you'd change your mind about my going to the Vegas meeting." Sob loudly, "Freddy loved Vegas. I'll probably be depressed the whole time there, but at least I won't try to jump down the elevator shaft like I might if I have to stay here in the office. Can I go, please?"

Do This . . .

Turn Tasks into Games. When your TOT refuses to approve a project you requested, try to make it so irresistibly fun that she won't be able say no. Let's say she nixes the idea of having a client appreciation party. In addition to making your case for the customer bonding that the party would yield, create a menu mock-up containing her favorite foods—or propose having it at her favorite restaurant. Always think about how, in fulfilling your desire, you could give your boss something she wants. You'll find her stubbornness might just melt faster than an ice-cream cone in August.

 DON'T DO THIS . . .

Remind Your TOT Who the Big Dog Is. When your boss won't let you put an espresso machine in the break room, press the issue so that she breaks down and gives in. Say: "Boss, have you forgotten that I won the coffee consumption competition last year, after I downed 31 cappuccinos in three hours? I mean, nobody knows coffee like I do. And I can tell you, the junk we serve in our break room would bring a water buffalo to tears. It has absolutely no kick and, no joke, that machine I want to order will enhance productivity. So let's order the Mean Beans Machine, pronto. Sign here."

Do This . . .

Use Flattery. If your TOT barricades every idea that you put forth, she isn't going to suddenly say, "Oh, what a lovely notion. Let me embrace your great idea and give you a big hug." No . . . she'll continue to squash you unless you cleverly make her think that your idea first came from her. It's unfortunate that you have to resort to this, but so is an intransigent TOT. So when you want to hire a temp to help with the backlog, say "You know, I've been thinking about your idea of getting some extra help to get this project done. It's an awesome solution. Who should I call?" If she denies ever suggesting it, say "I could have sworn it was your brainstorm. Well, it's a great idea, anyway, don't you think?"

 DON'T DO THIS . . .

Make Ultimatums Often. When your boss insists that you attend a meeting despite your e-mail documenting your need to be elsewhere, draw a few lines in the sand. Tell her, "Boss, either you let me skip the meeting or I'll just have to quit and become an Australian bounty hunter." If she points out that you aren't Australian, tell her, "Well I'll become one anyway. Just stay on my good side—my uncle's closest friend is in the CIA."

> **Do This ...**
>
> **Offer Choices.** Instead of posing your request as a Yes/No question, offer your TOT choices. In other words, don't ask, "Can we end the meeting early today?" Rather, ask, "Should we end the meeting at 4:00 PM, or at 4:30 PM?" If you have a particularly intractable boss, you can expand the options. "Or, should we have everyone complete the survey at their desks before they arrive, so that we can end at 3:00 PM?" Your TOT will feel immense decision-making power, so he won't have to assert it by saying no.

TOT-Busters Q&A

Question

At my company we have to work one evening a week. My boss sets the schedule and he's assigned me to work Tuesday nights, but that night doesn't fit with my schedule. He absolutely refuses to modify the schedule, no matter how many times I ask politely. And now, even when I've found several people who agreed to switch with me, he won't budge no matter how much I plead and beg. Any ideas?

Answer

Once you're locked into a battle of wills, it's difficult to get your boss to back down. Pushing harder, albeit politely, can easily take your TOT over the edge. Early intervention would have been the key. Next time, offer choices and solutions upfront, have a back-up plan, and you might be free every Tuesday.

Points to Remember

- Stubborn bosses fear losing face, losing control, or acquiring extra work by giving in.
- Some stubborn TOTs think leadership means inflexible, unyielding rule.
- Temper your boss's obstinacy by giving him choices, and having a back-up plan.
- Flatter your TOT's ideas, even though they're really yours, or a version of hers.
- Choose your words carefully when making requests, and listen intently, so you've allowed your TOT to be heard.

9

Tantrums

About Tantrums

IT'S 3:00 PM on Monday afternoon. You've been putting out fires all day—you even skipped lunch to cover the front desk—and now you're desperate for an afternoon cappuccino and muffin. You grab your wallet and head for the elevator down to the coffee shop, but your Terrible Office Tyrant (TOT) intercepts you as the doors open.

"Hey," she says, "where are you going?"

You can tell from her tone that getting a muffin is not what she has in mind for you. Still, you crave that caffeine blast and blueberry bun, so you blurt out the truth: "I'm going to get coffee." The next thing you know, you're back in your office with a stack of redlined reports and the promise of another late night at your desk, while your boss contacts you every five minutes to remind you of things you have on your plate (which, unfortunately, does not include a muffin). Then she bursts in again carrying an extra-large caramel macchiato in her fist, sloshing the foam onto your desk as she gesticulates.

Is it possible that your boss—the leader of your team—handles stress no better than a toddler going through the terrible twos? On closer inspection, does her behavior resemble that of a child throwing a tantrum?

But Why?

Your boss might look like a bona fide executive, but don't let the laptop and lapels fool you. Did your boss's emotional maturity terminate at age two? Is your seemingly adult boss really a TOT?

Why would a grown adult in a position of power throw tantrums reminiscent of toddlers being told "No!" in a checkout line? Is there any real difference between a fist-pounding manager and a screeching toddler sprawled on the floor, candy locked in her fist?

Unfortunately, one of the most glaring similarities between toddlers and TOT bosses is that when faced with a situation out of their control, they resort to rage and tantrums. Of course, bosses don't throw tantrums over candy . . . they scream and wail over missed sales numbers, budget cuts, and clashes with their bosses, Big TOTs.

Despite their age, bratty bosses are really just children inside. Many make a concerted effort to put a professional face on their emotions, but when they sense any threat to their power, their inner TOT says, "Wait a minute . . . . I'm the boss! I had better make it clear I'm the boss, and that things will happen my way in the future."

Once the TOT mentality kicks in, the professional façade disappears. Consider the parallels:

Toddler Tantrum Behavior	TOT Tantrum Behavior
She yells, "No, no, no, spinach is yucky! Noooooo!"	She yells, "No, no, no, don't you know how to write a proposal? You did it all wrong. Noooooo!"
He cries and stomps in defiance due to wrongs supposedly perpetrated by you: "*You* ate my cookie . . . where's my COOKIE?"	He loses it over your supposed shortcomings: "Because of you, we lost that account and now I'm going to pay for it! If the axe falls on me, it's *your* fault!"
Because you wouldn't let your child stay up late to watch TV, he stomps away from you and refuses cuddles.	Because you wouldn't give in to your TOT's third request this week for you to stay late, he marches out of your office and is curt.
He won't let you near his toys, because you always end up taking them from him.	He won't let you near his pet project because he prefers to let his "yes men" work on it.

What causes tantrums? TOTs and toddlers actually throw fits for the same reason—they can't assert their developing power and independence. Your little tyke and TOT occasionally find that their ability to master the world is limited, as it is with most mortal beings. This revelation, on top of their inability to communicate clearly, makes them frustrated and furious.

Also, TOTs and toddlers have little sense of their impact on others, few inhibitions, an inability to soothe themselves, and limited awareness that they're even erupting into an infantile rage. In fact, within minutes or hours, they can forget it ever happened and can become outright chummy (especially around 6:00 PM when you're getting ready to leave).

The Many Types of Tantrums

Tantrums come in a variety of flavors, depending on the trigger.

Bad News Blast

When your department misses a sales target, or drops the ball on a big deal with a client, or ends up in a situation where revenues, profits, or goals may be in jeopardy, the axe is likely to fall, and your tantrum-throwing TOT may swing it wildly.

Displaced Anger

Your boss may be angry—not at you directly—but at something bad or scary that happened earlier outside of work, and over which your TOT had no control. If your boss's girlfriend just broke up with him, you might get scolded for lingering in the break room. You were simply in the line of fire.

Heated Hand-Down

Fits can be triggered by something that a big boss just said, did, or took away. (Don't forget, TOT bosses usually have a TOT of their own to deal with.) Your boss may routinely handle stress and pressure by "sharing the love" with you.

Moody Monday

TOTs often have inexplicable, hair-trigger mood swings that crop up without warning. Your boss starts out as a virtual charmer on Monday morning, but morphs into a raging bull by afternoon. Mood swings can be set off by the most microscopic misunderstanding, or by basic "boo-boos" such as exhaustion, hunger, a long commute, a toothache, or the weight of a full day's work. Beware: Moody Monday can strike on any day of the week. Even Friday. (See Chapter 18, Mood Swings, for more on this.)

True TOT Tales

The Jelly Donut Incident

Mike worked as a technical writer at a software company in Boston. He came face-to-face with a TOT tantrum in his first week on the job. So much for the honeymoon period.

> I had just joined the team. On Friday mornings, they offered a generous spread of fresh donuts and bagels in the break room, and this was my first Friday morning event. While I don't usually eat junk food, I felt I had earned a treat that first week, so I grabbed two jelly donuts and put them on a paper plate.
>
> Within minutes, the staff filled the room, including the department head, Steve, who proudly sauntered in. Steve was initially all smiles, until suddenly his face turned beet red. In seconds, he was in a murderous rage, screaming, "Who took my jelly donuts?"
>
> I had already finished the first donut. The second had a substantial bite missing from the edge and bright red jam was oozing out onto my plate. I didn't want to get fired on the spot, so I covered the second unfinished jelly donut under my napkin, and rolled my chair behind my friend, Jeff. Jeff had a football-player build and had worked a few years at the company—a good person to hide behind.
>
> But hiding didn't end the pain: Steve continued to shriek and wave his arms until he tired out, leaving the room defiant, but donut-less.
>
> Steve's behavior was so outrageous it was almost comical. I could hardly believe that this grown man, who ran a $2 million division, could make such a public spectacle over donuts.
>
> From that moment on, the incident became known as the "donut tantrum." While my colleagues and I snorted with laughter whenever we recollected Steve's behavior, the donut

incident did traumatize me. Because of it, I spent the next few months learning less about the basics of my job than about the basics of handling Steve and his Oscar-worthy fits.

Even though Mike had only been on the job for a week, he passed his first TOT-taming hurdle. He reached out to his trusted colleagues after the tantrum subsided, and gained additional insights into dealing with Steve. From that point forward, Mike distanced himself from his diaper-ready director by identifying some of the triggers that instigated Steve's tendency to combust.

Mike learned how to manage his boss by trial-and-error, but you can take a short cut by adapting the toddler-rearing practices of savvy parents. Parents learn early how to minimize conditions that make their kids fussy. They know that when they forget to plan ahead, toddler trouble is sure to ensue.

TOT-Taming Tips: Tantrums

Certainly, smart moms know not to wheel their little cookie monsters down the snacks aisle at the grocery store when they are cranky and need a nap. But do you know what the equivalent "temper triggers" are for your boss? If you witness emotional infancy in the executive office, you can reign triumphant by avoiding the pitfalls and following some tried and true TOT-training advice.

 DON'T DO THIS . . .

Be Spontaneous. Ask your boss for a raise whenever the mood hits you, like the day after you accidentally hit her new convertible in the parking lot. You can corner her by the elevator when she's on her way to lunch, or block the door to the ladies' room when she's about to enter, or interrupt a meeting with potential clients. If the whim hits you first thing in the morning before she's had her coffee, go for it. When your boss says, "What makes you think you deserve a raise?" stare her in the eyes and say, "Hey, you know the reasons why I deserve a raise."

Do This ...

Plan Ahead. Know your boss's routines and preferences, including the best time of day and best day of the week to approach her. Show up to meetings on time, and bring your documentation—preferably reports with easy-to-read summaries, lots of colors, and three-dimensional pie charts. If your boss assigns you a brand-new task that could be challenging, consider the ultimate pacifier statements: "That will be the first thing on my to-do list." Or, "What a great idea! Thank you." Finally, where possible, give instant praise to any comments that are supportive.

 DON'T DO THIS ...

Fight a Tantrum with a Tantrum. When your boss gets snitty or critical with you, don't put up with it. For instance, if your boss starts complaining about your attendance record even though you've only missed one day in the past six months, say something like "Oh yeah? Says who?" If he raises his voice, say something even more assertive. Try: "I got 620 on my verbal SAT; what did *you* get?"

Do This . . .

Use CALM. CALM is an acronym that is useful for all TOT behavior, but especially tantrums. In the broadest sense, remaining calm even though your boss may provoke you is the best step you can take. For example, saying things like "That must make you very upset" or "How can I help with the backlog?" diffuses anger. A boss's blame can become apologetic shame if you handle it right. Here's an explanation of the handy acronym, CALM:

- Communicate—Keep the lines open, regularly.
- Anticipate—Know your timing: don't step into the "line of fire," and know what will put your boss at ease.
- Laugh—Humor is the great diffuser. Use it to bring down barriers.
- Manage—Be the voice of reason and manage up, using diplomacy and being a proactive problem solver.

 DON'T DO THIS . . .

Hang Around for the Show. Even if you're comfortable in your own cubicle, when you hear your boss ranting down the hall, rouse yourself from your nap and walk to where the action is. Enter his space and say, "Hey, que pasa?" Find a cushy chair, preferably one that rotates, make yourself cozy and wheel yourself right into the path of fire. If things get really tense, rotate around in your chair until you feel better, or make a big show of covering your ears so that your boss takes the hint.

Do This ...

Give Your Boss a Reverse Time-Out. You can't send your boss to his room when he goes ballistic, but you can maneuver to leave the scene yourself. Look at your watch, and say "I've got an important call scheduled that I need to get to. It could get us closer to that deal with the client. I hate to do this, but would you be willing to defer our conversation?" The key is to have ready a handful of legitimate excuses with which to leave the scene. Your departure will bring the pyrotechnics show to an end, giving your TOT ample time to settle down. He'll have time alone ... and time to think more clearly.

 DON'T DO THIS ...

Let the Fits Rip. No matter how abusive your boss becomes, there's some spiritual lesson you can glean. If you want to cultivate your humility (or precipitate your own psychotic breakdown), stick with the job no matter what happens. Spend days, months, or even years listening to your boss throw fits and being subjected to his ugly treatment of you. When things get nasty, stuff a donut in your mouth, and then try for another (ideally your boss's favorite jelly donut). Then count the minutes until Friday at 5:00 PM.

Do This . . .

Set Limits or Walk. If your current TOT isn't tamable, you're always free to walk. Remember, there's a big difference between putting up with outrageous, abusive behavior—which no employee should tolerate—and annoying little flare-ups that come and go. If you are dealing with an abusive boss, you should seek the counsel of a trusted friend or coworker. If the mistreatment gets worse, you might consider filing a formal complaint with your human resources department. Unfortunately, if things escalate to that point, you may be better off leaving.

On the other hand, if your boss can listen to reason, after he settles down, ask him if you can discuss the incident. Calmly suggest that "asking politely" will yield better results. Make sure not to point the finger at him; instead, focus on how his tantrum affected you. This gives him positive reinforcement for solving problems civilly.

TOT-Busters Q&A

Question

My TOT seems to go from peaceful harmony to pitiful harangue in just seconds. My therapist doesn't think he's bipolar, and I know it's impossible to take my TOT in for testing. Should I be worried?

Answer

This behavior actually is a common characteristic of TOT tantrum throwers. Nothing can be ruled out, but the unexpected nature of the tirade is a classic means to "shock and awe," making the event that much more robust and memorable. You should try to find the triggers for your boss's more harmonious moments. Figure out how to get him back in a good mood—and keep him there. Learning how to avoid the negative triggers is also a good idea. But remember, you can't control the external influences on him, so sometimes, it's just better to stay away when you can.

 Points to Remember

When you witness emotional infancy in the corner office, it may signal a need for "training pants." The key is to pick your battles. If your current TOT isn't tamable, you're always free to leave. But remember that TOTs run rampant in corporate America—and a new boss could be even more colicky than the old one.

To tame a TOT tantrum:

- Plan ahead.
- Create a distraction.
- Contain your reaction.
- Give your boss a reverse time-out.
- Walk if you have to.
- Remember the acronym CALM: Communicate, Anticipate, Laugh, and Manage.

10

Territorialism

About Territorialism

YOU'VE JUST BEEN assigned the entire Northeast sales region—the prime market for your industry. You are certain you will be able to increase your visibility and income working this route. What's more, you have another reason for your enthusiasm: the Northeast corridor is the territory that made your boss a star—and launched him onto the company's fast track.

This seems like a dream come true, until you find your Terrible Office Tyrant (TOT) is not nearly as happy about your assignment as you are. In his head, the Northeast corridor is still his territory.

He begins a rampage of criticism, constantly demanding updates—and trashing your plans. "You know, that's not how I did it when I had the Northeast." He undermines your efforts by reaching out to his old client contacts himself, and he gripes to senior management.

Your TOT's interference comes to a head in the weeks leading up to an important trade show. You spend days on the telephone, trying to set up client meetings, only to find your prime clients are claiming their schedules are booked. When you investigate, you find your TOT has already lined up appointments with them—without inviting you.

"I'm the one who made this territory what it is. I'm the experienced professional. So I stepped in," he says. At the end of your first quarter, your numbers confirm what you already know: you have been running in place, thanks to a boss who can't let go. The Northeast territory is quickly going south!

But Why?

What's going on here? This is a textbook case of a territorial TOT—and the proverbial "sandbox syndrome" is at play. Although he has moved on to new responsibilities, this TOT is unwilling to cede his old stomping grounds to anyone. The result is a turf war where anyone taking over the boss's old territory is at a distinct disadvantage.

The parallels to toddler behavior are striking. Picture a two-year-old with a new, adorable baby sister. The toddler has long given up his rattles and blankies, but as soon as the new baby arrives, he gathers up all these treasures and refuses to relinquish them. He doesn't really want them; he just doesn't want anyone else to have them.

Territorialism is all about defending one's stuff—be it emotional or physical—against those who'd try to muscle in. TOTs will defend office space, important relationships, keys to the supply closet, and even your time. Consider the parallel behavior.

Toddler Territorial Behavior	TOT Territorial Behavior
You are visiting family with your toddler. He eats less than half of his hot dog slices before giving up. When you offer the remaining slices to his little cousins, he reaches up and grabs them out of your hand, screaming "Mine!"	An important TOT from another department asks if you could help introduce his new employee to your team. As you begin the tour, your TOT arrives with a new pile of paperwork and insists you address it ASAP. "Tell her we're too busy to baby-sit over here," he sneers.
Your young kids come home from school with their art projects. Your son's drawing is placed above your daughter's on the refrigerator. As you turn your back, your daughter tapes her drawing over his. Your son gives both of you the silent treatment for six hours.	One of your colleagues was honored as September Employee of the Month on the wall behind the reception desk. When an employee from another department gets the honor for October, your TOT rips the display from the wall, snarling, "It's not October until Monday."
You are in the grocery store with your toddler, buying food for the entire family. With each item that goes into the cart, your child accuses you of not loving her enough to buy the cookies and ice cream that she wants.	You bring great cost-saving measures to your team meeting. Your TOT publicly accuses you of sucking up to the accounting manager, squealing mockingly, "If you love accounting so much, why don't you transfer over there?"
You spend hours getting ready to go out for a big party. You style your hair, choose just the right clothes and shoes. Your spouse says, "You look fantastic!" Your child, angry that you're going out for the first time in months, says, "You look like a poo poo head!"	You are singled out for praise at the staff meeting, even by Big TOT. Everyone loves your idea for a new customer strategy. And then your TOT speaks up, "Actually, I have concerns about this idea." He spends the rest of the meeting tearing you down.

What causes territorialism? It has its roots in the evolution of human behavior: he who can best gather and defend has the optimal chances for self-preservation.

Territorial TOT Types

So what makes your TOT display his territorial claims in the office setting? It stands to reason that the same skills he would use to survive preschool would serve him well in the hand-to-hand combat of corporate life. The goal is to get stuff—and keep it. The motivations can vary.

Threats from Others

A TOT who senses that someone is going to try to take something that was once hers—ranging from her old office, to a key account, to her lucky coffee cup—will be inspired to defend it should someone else show interest. Old instincts die hard. She may have given up old territory when she was promoted, but she still sees it as hers.

Competitiveness

Often, territorialism is nothing more than a show of force. Your TOT doesn't really need you to be in your office, working 100 percent of the time on his assigned tasks. But if he shows he can control every minute of your day, while holding off other managers' attempts to use your talents, he displays his power. Consider it sibling rivalry—TOT style.

Arrogance

For some TOTs, life and work are a game where whoever has the biggest pile of toys wins. Other TOTs must leave her turf alone, and if they dare to venture into her sandbox, she will see to it that they end up in a sandstorm.

Insecurity

Despite his advanced position in the company, your TOT may worry his spot is not secure. Therefore, any attempt to weaken him by reducing his cache of stuff is to be fought off at all costs. Any loss of prestige is one tiny step closer to a pink slip.

True TOT Tales

Tech Territory Troubles

Marcy was a newbie in the IT department at a large corporation. Fresh out of MIT, she was well schooled in the latest technology. But when she came to her first job, she found her skills actually created problems for her. Her TOT boss saw the newcomer as an intruder, rather than a team member. Here's Marcy's story:

> *I was really nervous when I started my first job, but I did everything I could to be helpful. I made sure my boss and colleagues were briefed on the new technologies I was familiar with and how my skills could be leveraged to help the team. I thought I was showing everyone that I was a great hire. Instead, I was opening myself up to a huge headache.*
>
> *My boss, Janice, had been with the company 10 years. She had a degree in computer programming, but in this age of light-speed tech changes, her education was outdated. My experience was more of a threat to her than a benefit.*
>
> *As a result, she looked for every opportunity to trip me up. She tossed the most impossible assignments my way, often with a comment like: "Let's see the MIT genius fix this!" Janice seemed to be rooting for me to fail. I knew she needed me to pull*

my weight with her team. But she seemed to be undermining me. I was at a loss.

So I asked around discreetly at work: What was I doing wrong? Several people in the department told me that Janice feared I might threaten her position.

I immediately changed my behavior. Instead of talking up my own skills, I focused on Janice's contributions. She had great strategic and organizational abilities, and I made sure she knew these were critical to my work. I also put in extra hours training her on short cuts to our new software. She did have a good mind for IT and learned quickly.

This was the ticket. She stopped making it her mission to thwart me and actually started to thank me once in a while. She never became my biggest fan, but the shift in her attitude made my first job a lot more tolerable.

- -

Marcy learned there's more to getting ahead than having the right skills or even doing a good job. You must survey the "deeper sensitivities" of a position. Marcy learned to manage her boss's territorialism and make her own job much more pleasant.

TOT-Taming Tips: Territorialism

What can you do to keep your TOT's territorial instincts under control? Often, it's a question of identifying—and then, avoiding—the triggers. Many times, the TOT will react to some small encroachment that he fears could turn into a full-fledged border war. If you can keep triggers to a minimum, you can keep your TOT from feeling like he's under attack. And, of course, if you're looking for a fight, you can always just camp out in his office. Here are some more Do's—and Don'ts—to consider:

DON'T DO THIS …

Advertise Mistakes. Walk with your TOT back to his office to rehash a special staff gathering that has gone poorly. As you walk past your colleagues, proclaim loudly, "Well, that meeting sure was career suicide for you! That guy from Corporate really dissed your whole agenda."

Do This …

Keep Things Moving. Did something go badly for your TOT? She will feel less threatened by everyone if you help her look ahead, not back. Talk up her skills, and link them to upcoming projects. Keep your mutual energy focused on the tasks ahead—with a fresh outlook for both of you. Identify areas where your TOT and your team will have a significant impact in the days and weeks ahead.

 DON'T DO THIS …

Grab the Spotlight. Make sure to toot your own horn, often. If you can do something better than anyone in the office, especially your boss, make sure every employee knows about it. Send out e-mails, start a blog, and on casual day, wear a T-shirt that says, "I'm with Stupid" when you have a scheduled lunch meeting with your TOT. Gather your colleagues in the conference room for a demo of your hotshot computer skills. "See, I can do this, and I can do that. And, oh, this is really cool … look, boss!"

Do This ...

Promote Your Boss. Talk up your team—and your boss. By diverting the spotlight from yourself, you are avoiding the notion that you are trying to lay claim to your boss's turf. When you are praised for good work, be sure to say how your boss supported your efforts—and how his management skills created an environment for success. Keep communications flowing regularly. Do not give him cause to worry that you are encroaching on his hard-won pile of toys.

 DON'T DO THIS ...

Be a Full-Time Volunteer. Donate all of your time to the other TOTs in your company. If you get bored with your own job, offer your services to the struggling department head down the hall. She'll be thrilled to have your help. Be sure to leave a sticky note on your chair, in case your boss hasn't seen you for three weeks, saying "I'm over in the marketing department helping them with their systems project. The boss over there is really nice. Drop by and say hi when you're bored." Then consider preparing an e-mail to all department heads saying you are looking for work.

Do This ...

TOT First, Others Second. Keep the priorities of your TOT at the forefront. When crafting your daily, weekly, and monthly schedule, review your TOT's priorities for the period and be sure your actions dovetail. Volunteering for team projects is great, but make sure you've gone above and beyond the call of duty for her before taking on new work. When asked for help by another department, refer the request to your TOT for approval.

 DON'T DO THIS ...

Take Over. If you end up in a position once held by your boss, make sure that you enact sweeping changes to make that job your own. Announce to everyone, "I have great new ideas on how we can really rock and roll! We need to ditch all the old, tired methods and revamp our entire concept." Bring a large pail and shovel to show you're ready to play in his once-coveted sandbox.

Do This ...

Let Your TOT Mentor You. When stepping into an area where your TOT is an expert, tap into her expertise. You'll get great insights while learning—and respecting—those territorial borders. Learn to make changes by suggesting improvements on her methods, rather than outright rejection of her model. Remember that no matter what, your boss will likely consider her way of doing things as the best way. With a collegial relationship, she'll begin to see that you have some fresh new insights to offer.

TOT-Busters Q&A

Question

I've been in my job for three years. I spent the first two learning the ropes, but now I'm starting to be valued across departments. Other managers are asking me to take part in projects that affect our area, where I could add my expertise and help the company. The problem is my boss is loading me up with busy work, so I'm never free to participate in teams that would actually help our department. I feel like I'm not being viewed as a team player. What can I do?

Answer

Consider how a territorial TOT views this situation. He has spent two years training you, so he considers you his investment and he doesn't want to lose you to others. Your first line of loyalty is to your boss, but you can step out of the fray by having the managers talk to each other. They will likely speak about your value on their project teams. You can also suggest a joint meeting or lunch with you, your boss, and other project leaders and/or managers present. But also let your TOT know the value your contributions bring to the company, how it indirectly (or directly) helps your boss, and how it satisfies your need to grow professionally.

 Points to Remember

- Map out your TOT's turf. It's easier to respect boundaries when you know where they are.
- Don't be a glory-seeker. Respect his accomplishments, and learn from his experience.

- Learn to juggle multiple responsibilities if they cross into other departments. Keep your priorities on your main job, and reassure your TOT that you will not lose sight of what she hired you to do.
- Always keep your TOT in the loop to provide reassurance.

11

Whining

About Whining

IT'S BEEN A LONG DAY and you're cramming on a killer deadline. Everyone on the team is focused on getting a proposal in order for a critical, high-visibility project. It's a huge job and no one is sure it can be done, but the group pulls together a full court press to make it happen.

The office is quiet, yet buzzing with the low hum of hard work. Heads are bent over keyboards. The mood is serious and intense. The sun is setting and shadows are falling across your cubicle when your Terrible Office Tyrant (TOT) makes her appearance.

Her own work is on hold until your team finishes the proposal, and instead of sitting quietly and harmlessly in her office, she has emerged to wander the corridors. She approaches your desk.

"Isn't this done yet? I feel like I've been waiting forever," she barks.

"We're making progress, boss. Should be done soon," you say, hoping to placate her.

No luck. She pulls back and begins to pace the aisle. "I don't see why it's taking this long. I shouldn't have to wait like this. It's not acceptable that I should wait," she drones.

Her voice begins to rise, carrying across the sea of cubicles. "Other departments have their paperwork finished," she continues. "Why isn't our paperwork finished? The other managers are already done and are out having a drink and celebrating—and I'm stuck here."

Your TOT wanders to the next cubicle, continuing to express her woe at the upper levels of her vocal register. Before you can cover your ears, you practically hear the glasses in the break room shatter. What just happened? You have just experienced the "Attack of the Whiner."

But Why?

Whining is rampant in the toddler world. Small children are utterly dependent and often resentful of the fact that so little is in their control. In an attempt to manipulate grownups to their will, toddlers will often whine. That high, nasal, continuous cry of a young child will often cause adults to do anything requested, if only to get that infernal noise to stop.

TOTs are no strangers to this behavior. Whining is a way to get what they want—be it comfort and support or results and achievement. Many a subordinate will hop to it, if not to stop the TOT from whining, then as an act of career protection.

Toddler whining and TOT whining have a lot in common, often sharing identical triggers:

Whining Toddler Behavior	Whining TOT Behavior
You're on the phone and your toddler comes into the room and looks like her cat died. "Mommy, I need a snack. Mommy, Mommy!" She is mopey, grabs your arm, leg, then your phone, until you hang up and surrender to stop the tireless chants.	You're on the phone with an important client. Your boss comes into the office and tries to get your attention. He waves, gestures, whispers, scribbles on sticky notes, placing them on your computer screen. He returns to his office and sends you e-mails in ALL CAPS, until you hang up and let him grouse in person.
You are choosing a checkout counter, but the only open register is the one with candy. Your toddler sees the candy. "I want candy! Candy!"	It's budget time. Seated around the conference table, everyone is making hard budget choices. Your TOT grumbles, "I don't know why we can't just get more money. We can't cut this. More money!"
It's bedtime. Your toddler is tired and cranky, but refuses to go to bed. He follows you around the house, instead of going to bed. "Mommy, I need my teddy. Mommy, my tummy hurts. I'm thirsty."	It's quitting time. The boss is out of her office, wandering the halls, poking into cubicles and complaining. "Where's the budget report? When are final numbers coming in? When is tomorrow's meeting?"
She has to complete an art project for preschool. The assignment: glue various paper shapes onto cardboard. You cut out the shapes. You prepare the cardboard. You open the glue stick. Your toddler sits before the project, glue stick in hand, and whines, "Noooooo! Mommy, you do it!"	Your TOT has to write a memo to Super TOT, outlining the accomplishments of the division. You prepare the research. You outline the report text. You load the materials onto your TOT's computer. He sits before it, frozen, saying, "Why do I have to do everything around here?"

Whining is common in small children because they are largely at the mercy of adults. It is often the first indication a toddler has of his own power: "Sure, the grownups may be bigger and stronger and have the car keys, but if I whine long enough, I could still get my way."

Unfortunately, "success breeds success"—which makes whining a handy habit for toddlers. After all, it is the single best way to get a grown-up to do what you want. For exactly that reason, whining often extends into adulthood. Your TOT, struggling with feelings of inadequacy, fear, loneliness, or fatigue, may reach back for the tactic that never let him down as a toddler.

Varieties of Whining

Why does your TOT whine? There are four major catalysts.

Powerlessness

Whiners unleash their best howls when they feel powerless or threatened. Whining is a tried and true way to influence people and swing them to your point of view—even if the agreement is only made so the whining will stop.

No Fuel in the Tank

Like toddlers, TOTs revert to whining when their energy is sapped. It's quite possible that when your boss is whining, he may just be tired or hungry. Low-energy whiners usually seem perfectly normal most of the day and transform into sniveling brats after 4:00 PM. Sometimes these whiners will make a special appearance right before lunch.

Loneliness

Whining is often a bid for attention. Your whining TOT—especially the one who whines about her personal life—may be trying to draw your sympathy and bond with you.

Disappointment

In toddlers, whining is often a reaction to the realization that things are not going to go their way. Faced with disappointment, this can happen in TOTs as well. Your TOT may whine simply to vent frustration and dismay.

True TOT Tales

A Captive Audience

Rita was a star on a customer service team for an insurance firm in the Midwest. Her job required her to be at her desk and available by phone or e-mail for much of the day. As a result, she was almost always in her cubicle and therefore easy to find. Due to the nature of her job, Rita was known to be a good listener. But her patience and sympathy were to be severely tried by her TOT boss.

> *Everyone knows that 90 percent of good customer service is being a good listener. Many times, all the customer wants to do is vent and have someone lend a sympathetic ear. That's why I'm good at my job.*
>
> *My boss, the manager for the region, began to take my job skill as an invitation to bend my ear whenever he pleased. He'd show up at my cubicle throughout the day to whine about whatever was on his mind. He complained about everything, from his lousy love life to his lemon of a luxury car to his "measly" bonus package.*

It was right after the annual industry convention that things went from bad to worse. My boss had traveled to the convention, but he had to fly coach while his superiors got to fly first class. He was especially peeved when his supervisor waved, smiling to him from behind the curtain of that section. He whined about this incessantly for a month!

Finally, I had to do something to change the dynamic. Even though it went against my instincts, whenever he showed up at my desk, I did my best to convey through my body language that I wasn't really listening. I continued to do things around my desk, moving my paperwork, checking my e-mail.

It felt strange to me, but eventually, he seemed to get the picture: I was not going to be a personal sounding board for him any more. He cut back significantly on his visits to my desk and his whining overall. And I didn't get fired.

Rita made an important discovery: Whining is a habit that can be changed. Her TOT was whining to her because she was creating an inviting atmosphere—she was staying in one place and greeting the whiner with her undivided attention.

But when she stopped providing the nonverbal approval on a consistent basis, the whiner was able to pick up on the signals and change his behavior. Rita was able to help this TOT outgrow a bad habit. She had become a Class A TOT tamer.

TOT-Taming Tips: Whining

Whining is a behavior most TOTs (with help from TOT tamers) can control, if given the proper mindset, instructions, and encouragement. Consistency is key, no matter how annoying the whining gets. TOT Tamers must be willing to demonstrate clear expectations and not get drawn into the emotions of the moment, as seen in these tips:

DON'T DO THIS ...

Deliver a 5 O'Clock Surprise. Wait until the waning hours of the work day, when your TOT is famous for recapping her day's problems one by one. Strut into your boss's office and alert her to a crisis you've been sitting on all day. Demand that she look at the information right away. Interrupt her whiny recitations whenever possible, reminding her your issue is paramount, and go over the impending decision repeatedly.

Do This ...

Watch the Clock. Remember that TOTs, like toddlers, get cranky as the day wears on. Asking them to do something new or important late in the day is dangerous and may bring on a whine attack. Instead, try to keep late-day surprises to a minimum, presenting new information to your TOT at the start of the day, when she's fresh. Look for body language clues and be prepared to back off if you see tell-tale signs such as rubbing of the eyes, repetitive yawns, or distractibility.

 DON'T DO THIS ...

Let the Cupboard Go Bare. If your TOT's favorite candy bar is the last one in the vending machine, buy it and savor it. Don't bother alerting administration for a refill. After all, it's not your job to keep the troops supplied with food. You have work to do. You can't be bothered with other people's hunger issues, and certainly not his. While you're at it, drain the last of the coffee and scoop up the sugar packets to keep in a stash in your desk drawer. Let the whines begin!

Do This . . .

Cater to Her Needs. Help keep the boss fed at long meetings because hungry TOTs are whining TOTs. Pay attention to the meal schedule, including snacks, and you'll head off many complaint sessions. Is there a meeting scheduled for 4:00 PM? Bring cookies. Is the team working late on a last-minute project? Be proactive and order a pizza. You could run into 30 minutes of exasperating grousing if you enter his office before lunch at 11:30 AM.

 DON'T DO THIS . . .

Pile It On! Barge into your TOT's office and bring as many items requiring his attention as possible. Slap them on his desk, one after the other. Write in red on each cover sheet "URGENT!" and "ASAP!" With each armful of paperwork you leave in his inbox, say, "Wow, this is really piling up. Look at this tower. Quite a stack you've got here, boss!"

Do This . . .

Give the Boss Some Space. Don't overwhelm your TOT with your project deliverables. If you must bring a number of them to her, you should prioritize them—or space them out. That approach may offer the added benefits of better feedback and a more positive response. Whining fits may emerge when the boss is faced with huge expectations and little sense of how to be successful. Head this off and its whiny aftermath by finding the right pace at which to submit your projects.

 DON'T DO THIS ...

Whine Together. When your boss drops by your cubicle and starts in on his daily rant, join in the fun with a whining duet. Don't be afraid to try different styles: country, classic rock, or R&B. Soon, you and the boss have got a good whining groove that can ripple throughout the office floor, causing ears to perk up through the building. Just imagine this future Top 40 smash:

Your TOT	"My budget is too small, and my boss plays favorites."
You	"Well, my computer's outdated and someone stole my Post-Its®."
Together	"It's always someone else's fault, and we just hate it!"

Do This ...

Send a "Busy" Signal. In situations when your boss seems like she's ready to whine, give her verbal and nonverbal indications that you're not going to offer your full attention.

Let her know you are on deadline for a project that she requested. Keep eye contact to a minimum. Excuse yourself to take phone calls or to check for "an important" client e-mail. Keep your ears open to make sure her rant is trivial. If it's serious, drop what you are doing and give her your undivided attention. (Before you give your boss the brush-off, make sure you check out Chapters 3 and 19 on *Demanding* and *Neediness*. Whining can be an outgrowth of either trait, so it helps to understand what lurks behind all the nagging!)

TOT-Busters Q&A

Question

My boss is generally reasonable in the morning, but at the daily 4:30 PM staff meeting, he becomes a royal pain. After working hard all day, we file in and have to listen to him complain about every little thing we do wrong, without any guidance on how we can do better. Most of us dread staff meetings. What can we do?

Answer

The problem you're encountering is likely one of timing. When your TOT's blood sugar has dropped in the late afternoon, he loses his grip on adult behavior. You have several options.

Consider adding snacks to the late afternoon meeting to reenergize for the final push of the day. Try for snacks that contain protein—avoid rich foods or sugary treats, unless you can wrap up before the sugar crash hits. Another option is to move the late meeting to an earlier time when the boss is not as worn out. Ask him: "Could this meeting be earlier in the day, when we all have more energy and you'd have our undivided attention? It's a critical opportunity for us to get your feedback."

 Points to Remember

- Be aware of the time. If whining occurs at specific times, direct your tougher conversations to better times.
- Don't feed into the whining. Matching a whine with another whine just adds fuel to the fire. Deflect and defuse the whining with calm conversation and, where possible, humor.
- Consider energy levels. Snacks can be seen as a generous offer that also chills out a whiny TOT.
- Head off whining by giving information and feedback to your boss consistently. If he doesn't have to ask for it, he'll be less whiny.

II

Little Lost Lambs

SOME DAYS, YOUR Terrible Office Tyrant (TOT) behaves more like a confused or anxious little kid than like a little devil. While meek may seem preferable to boisterous, that kind of high-maintenance boss can be simply exasperating. When your TOT wanders around aimlessly or fearfully, you can't exactly hold her hand, wipe her nose, and tell her everything is going to be okay.

However, you can provide support and direction—to keep your boss focused—and maintain your sanity. You can't afford to let a Little Lost Lamb run your department into the ground—or make your job a confusing tangle. You're better off taking action than hiding in the corner and sucking your thumb.

As they mature, kids need guidance to outgrow traits such as neediness, fickleness, and forgetfulness, while overcoming fears of the unknown. Your boss may need a similar type of support to succeed. Although your TOT's peers should fill that void, it doesn't happen as much as it should. And since you'll have to deal with a fearful, moody, or confused boss, you have much to gain if you can step in and help out, or "manage up."

By supporting your manager's efforts to overcome these child-ish traits, you are making your work life less stressful, while positioning yourself for advancement. Although some of these quirks will try your patience, your TOT-taming techniques will work wonders.

This section of *Tame Your Terrible Office Tyrant* covers the classic traits of those Little Lost Lambs. Each chapter includes a look at how TOTs and toddlers behave similarly; a real-life story about how an employee like you dealt with a challenging boss; and a set of useful TOT-Taming Tips.

12

Endless Questioning

About Endless Questioning

AT THE END of the month, your company is downsizing to a smaller office. It's your job to oversee the move of both personnel and equipment into the more modest building. It's a challenging job, involving coordination of multiple phases of moving, and a slim budget.

What's more, it is a time-sensitive process. Another company has already contracted to take over your firm's old digs. At the end of the month, you have to be in your new space or you'll be out on the street.

So far, your biggest problem is not the logistics of the move, but the constant interrogation from your Terrible Office Tyrant (TOT). Some days, it seems you spend half your time answering her questions:

- Where will my office be in the new building?
- What day is the move again?
- What is the view from my new office window?
- What day will I have to move my stuff?
- Is there same-day dry cleaning nearby?

- Where will the coffee machine be located?
- Are you sure we'll move that day?
- Where's the closest car rental place?

The questions are constant. Sometimes, your TOT sends e-mails:

Hi. Has anyone alerted our vending machine supply man? Because even a few days without microwave popcorn will be bad for morale. Can someone follow up on this, pronto, and confirm that the popcorn will be there on Monday ... in writing? And are you at the new offices now? Anyway, let me know. Thanks.

Sometimes, she sends voice mails:

Hi ... got a few questions. Will I get a new office chair when we move and will it recline? Did you make sure you kept the space plan locked up, and when can I see it? Oh ... did our staff get our fair share of space? In fact, how many cubes versus offices did we get? Hmm ... actually, can someone make sure I get a high-back chair with a headrest? Thanks.

Sometimes she resorts to stopping by your office:

Hi. I left you a couple voice mails a half hour ago, so I thought I'd better visit. Is there a problem with the new offices? Any problem on those special chairs? Is my office ready yet?

And finally, sometimes she simply runs into you in the hall.

I was just thinking about your move project. Remind me. . . . When are we moving?

But Why?

What's happening? It's the endless question syndrome. Like a young child who asks you a rapid string of questions from "Is there a little man in every traffic light?" to "Where do fish sleep?" and even, "Where does the refrigerator light go when I shut the door?" you get a constant barrage of queries as she tries to make sense of an overwhelming environment.

Consider the parallels:

Questioning Toddler Behavior	Questioning TOT Behavior
Every night before bedtime, your child gets mysteriously inquisitive and seemingly brilliant. "Why is the sky blue?" he asks. You explain the basic idea, but you get nowhere. "Yes, but why is it blue?" he demands. "Why not red or yellow or green? Why not purple?"	At 6:30 PM as you're packing up to go home, your TOT swings by and waxes philosophical: "Who invented the 40-hour work week?" Although you joke, "Someone who obviously didn't work here," she barely hears you. "Why isn't it an even 50? Why couldn't we do that?"
It's the middle of summer. Your toddler's birthday is in January, but she asks, "Is my birt'day here yet?" You patiently show her the calendar, but the next day, she asks, "Is today my birt'day?"	It's the middle of a crunch period. Your TOT drops by on his way out at 4:30 PM, asking "Are we done yet?" You give a quick status update and he leaves. He reappears at 8:00 AM with the same question, "Are we done yet?"
To get some quiet time, you give your daughter a doll you've stashed away for a special occasion. You settle down to read in the next room. But within minutes, you hear whimpers and then, "Why won't Sally sing? Is she sick? Can't you make her sing?!"	You're finally getting some work done when you hear loud thumps and a few choice words. You run over to find your TOT kicking his printer. "Why doesn't this work? Do you have this problem? Do you know how to fix the darn thing?"

Questioning Toddler Behavior	Questioning TOT Behavior
You're late for a Saturday appointment. You've got your toddler covered. You pause to kiss him before dashing out. He yells, "Wait! When are you coming home? Soon? Tomorrow? When, mommy?"	You're about to leave for a week on vacation. Your e-mail is clear and your projects are covered by colleagues. Your TOT comes by. "Are you really going to be gone for the entire week? Do you get back next Friday or Monday? Will you have e-mail access? Are you taking your cell?"

While toddlers have an innocence to their endless questions, TOTs often use the questions for a tactical advantage. Toddlers truly need their questions answered to better understand the universe or just to have a conversation with you. The endlessly questioning TOT may have more sophisticated motives.

Answering Questions Behind Endless Questioning

Why all the *whys*?

Micromanagement

The constant questions may signal a lack of trust in the job you are doing. If your TOT constantly asks you for minute details on your work progress, she may still want you on a short leash.

Deflection

How well is your TOT doing his job? The barrage of questions from the corner office may be the way he deflects attention from his own performance onto that of others or onto other topics.

Fear

Many bosses have anxiety when they can't comprehend something, or are not experts on every subject. They worry that the knowledge possessed by others will somehow eventually haunt them. Consequently, they are on a constant search for any and all knowledge. They fear that the one little thing they don't know will mean their permanent demise.

Loneliness

A young toddler finds comfort in the repetitive, soothing sound of your voice. If your TOT constantly follows you around with incessant questions, she may want to avoid isolation at all costs (the higher up you go, the lonelier it is).

Curiosity

Some bosses, like children, have an endless thirst for knowledge. Their intellectual curiosity is on overdrive because of the satisfaction and stimulation they receive from constant learning.

True TOT Tales

The Case of the Curious TOT

Jessica trained as a biomedical researcher. She joined a mid-sized pharmaceutical company, where she developed new product ideas for the firm. Jessica ran into trouble when her boss's manager began taking an interest in the biomedical details of the products he was supposed to sell. Here's Jessica's story:

> *I have always been a science nerd. So it was no surprise that I ended up as a professional scientist. But my world changed*

significantly when I left academia for a private sector job. I found managers in the pharmaceutical companies often rose through the sales ranks, not Research and Development.

I was helping to sort data on a potential new product when I first encountered Hal, my boss's manager. I was surprised to see him walk into my office. Most of the time, the execs don't bother to mix with the lab coats. But there he was. And he wanted me to explain the pros and cons of the potential new product—right now.

It was a complicated product, but I did my best. I gave him general descriptions, but he wanted details. He pressed me for the specifics on the chemistry, the makeup of the research trials, the history of the drug's classification status. I gave him more and more data, but that just seemed to make matters worse. It was all gibberish to him. He grew frustrated and walked off.

This went on for several weeks. I was on a tight deadline to get data ready for a major presentation, but Hal would not leave me alone to finish the job. He would show up, asking a string of questions. After I gave him an hour of my time, he would leave—still unsatisfied. And now I was also getting voice mail messages, phone calls at home, and questions via his PDA.

I asked around and found that Hal was under pressure to show more scientific knowledge than he had previously done. The company was looking to promote managers who had sales skills and a medical background. He was stressed because he was not a scientist. Hal feared this might cost him his job. I realized his questioning was a response to a threat from above, not because he didn't trust me.

So I took it upon myself to create a personalized tutorial for Hal. I began with some BioChem 101 notes and then sent him a series of memos outlining each concept, building his store of knowledge. He still stops by when he has a specific question, but now he has the foundation to understand the answer.

What happened here? Jessica was able to deal with her boss's manager's shortcomings and fear by asking a few basic questions of her own. As a result, she was able to help him out while giving herself a break from his incessant questioning. She also took the time to anticipate many of his questions, which made things much easier for both of them.

TOT-Taming Tips: Endless Questioning

Why do some bosses ask so many questions? How can you deal with TOTs who are full of questions? Would you like some TOT-Taming Tips to help you fend off your boss's curiosity? Is that enough questions? Are you sure? Okay, here are some Do's and Don'ts for dealing with TOTs who have more questions than answers.

 DON'T DO THIS . . .

Hold Back. Guard information closely. When your TOT asks questions, respond, "That's on a need-to-know basis." Suggest that a vast trove of data exists in your office, but that you are unwilling to share it. Tell curious TOT that for proprietary and career indispensability reasons, you keep a small circle of "insiders." Place a motion detector by your desk drawers.

Do This . . .

Over-Inform. Make it a habit to routinely send updates to your TOT, such as weekly e-mails. Anticipate questions she might ask. Organize regular meetings designed to keep your TOT in the loop. If she complains about being inundated, at least you've quelled the problem—"captured the initiative"—for the time being.

 DON'T DO THIS ...

Research Everything Asked. Work incessantly to answer each and every one of your TOT's questions, especially rhetorical ones. For example, if your TOT says, "I wonder if sending the proposal by Pony Express would have been faster than that so-called rapid overnight service," immediately conduct a Web search to determine the actual cost of that shipping method.

Do This ...

Keep Your Focus. Remain fixed on overall business goals. Your TOT may ask questions that inadvertently distract you. Although you'll need to acknowledge her inquiries, redirect the focus toward the pressing business tasks at hand. When she ponders, "Ever wonder what it'd be like if we painted the office fire-engine red?" consider: "That'd be interesting. Speaking of interesting, what'd you think of the client proposal I sent you this morning?"

 DON'T DO THIS ...

Argue the Point. Respond to irrelevant questions in a loud, aggressive way. Begin as many responses as possible with

"That's a lame question!" Continue on, accusing your TOT of wasting valuable billable hours with his tiresome, inane questions. Then be ready to respond to one final question: "Nice show, Rick. . . . Now can you kindly give me your keys to the office?"

Do This . . .

Force a "Mind Chuckle." It's okay to laugh off endless questions, as long as you do it in your head. A little humor—a Levity Lens of your own—can reduce some of the stress of rapid-fire questioning. Keep a mental tally of the number of legitimate questions your boss asks you versus the number of "Where does that other sock go?" or "Why does spam exist?" type of questions. Just as a toddler can be funny in his ongoing quest for knowledge, you can find internal humor in your TOT's endless ruminations. (If appropriate, however, always try some external, polite levity—you'd be surprised how it can shift the dynamics.)

 DON'T DO THIS . . .

Freak Out. Dust off your drama skills and make a scene. If you're surrounded by a pack of TOTs in the break room, create a crisis. As questions torpedo toward you, just fall on the floor, flail your arms and legs, and speak in loud, unintelligible phrases. If that doesn't work, try to imitate the sounds of farm animals, such as cows, pigs, and roosters. A donkey's "hee-haw" usually ends the questioning, but often attracts men with nets.

Do This . . .

Stay Calm. Not every question must have an answer. Sometimes, a question just needs an active listener because the TOT wishes to vent. If your TOT's questions are not business-related, listen politely and engage in some non-committal small talk. In other words, you can sometimes allow your TOT to answer his own questions.

TOT-Busters Q&A

Question

My office is located right next to the executive suite. My boss pops in as often as three times an hour to ask me questions. Sometimes, they're work-related, such as how am I progressing on a project or when do we have our next scheduled meeting? and other times, her questions are personal, such as how did I spend my weekend? What can I do?

Answer

To reduce the number of interruptions, first be sure you are meeting frequently with your TOT and updating her thoroughly on all projects. If you are already doing this, then use nonverbal cues to show that you are busy when she drops by.

Should the disruptions continue, consider closing your office door for short periods of time throughout the day to accomplish your work, and "apply as necessary!" That should send a signal that you need some private time to get your work done—and if you're questioned about it—explain that very point. As for the personal questions . . . give short, bland answers, such as, "Oh, not much," or "It was nice, how was your weekend?" and so on.

 Points to Remember

- Preemptive answers are the best way to curtail endless questioning. Take the initiative; the more your boss knows in advance, the less he will pester you with questions—and the more he will trust you.
- Constant questioning can often be held off by regularly scheduled briefings. You'll also have your ducks in a row.
- Give some thought to what's behind all the questioning. Not every question requires an answer.
- Keep smiling. Use an internal Levity Lens to see the TOT/toddler parallels, and remember, a light-hearted comment can often disarm rapid-fire questioning.

13

Fantasy World

About Fantasy World

YOU WALK INTO the conference room for a meeting where your boss is beaming. "I'm going to senior management with an exciting announcement. Due to the amazing success we had last year with the trial launch of our perfumed insecticide cream, InsectaSpice, I'm going to ask for a new budget for the official launch this year," your Terrible Office Tyrant (TOT) declares at the staff meeting.

You simply can't believe your ears. Your TOT wants to resurrect this buggy bomb during staff layoffs and a spiraling business climate. It was the fly in the ointment for the CEO last year, due to product recalls and bad press that almost sank your firm and your TOT along with it.

You wonder how such a dismal failure could end up back in play—and so, you cautiously inquire about the CEO's view. "Wow, that's . . . interesting news. You got the nod on this?"

He says, "I'll lock this thing up. I'm sure senior management will see that it's just what we need for our revenue situation. They'll let bygones be bygones. I mean, let's face it, the 3,472 consumer e-mails we got in two days was a record—and valuable feedback. That's what I call good work, team. And it's just the beginning!"

The strangest thing about this new development isn't that your TOT distorts the story—it's that he seems to believe it. He's truly proud of his failed product and won't let go. You see him headed once more into Fantasy Land until he gets a reality check from Big TOT.

But Why?

While you might expect kids to fantasize about being superheroes, that scenario doesn't seem as likely when the caped crusader is your 49-year-old boss. And yet, like kids, many TOTs live in an imaginary world characterized by distorted interpretations of reality. Perhaps your boss specializes in paranoia, fearing that her staff members are shiftless bums. He may picture himself as a stand-up comedian. Or maybe he thinks he's a shoo-in for the United States's Most Admired Executives list. Let's consider the similarities between how TOTs and toddlers create fantasy worlds:

Toddler Fantasy Behavior	TOT Fantasy Behavior
Your toddler won't go to sleep because a "boogeyman with seven eyeballs lives under the bed."	Your boss won't let you take on any interesting duties because she thinks ambitious employees are boogeymen, waiting to steal away her job.
He wraps a towel around his neck and runs through the house screaming, "I'm a bird, I'm a rocket, I'm Super Tom!" When he trips and falls flat on his face, he starts to cry, until you remind him of his superpowers, at which point he leaps up, yelling, "I'm a bird."	He becomes a superhero, gaining his powers from lifting indecipherable jargon from old magazines. He has the ability to "impress" everyone with knowledge like, "Regardless of the ADQM bandwidth, we need proactive initiatives to ensure robust NTP viability and scalability."

Toddler Fantasy Behavior	TOT Fantasy Behavior
She sneaks into your closet and plays dress-up to be a businesswoman like you.	He buys a monogrammed shirt and bow tie like the CEO and believes he's suddenly more important.
Your child grabs your elbow and insists that you come watch him build a skyscraper "as tall as the ceiling!" as you're paying bills.	Your TOT calls you while you're on deadline to show you a U.S. map on the wall with 647 future locations pinned into cork. But you still only have two offices.

TOTs retreat into fantasy because they've discovered that reality has its limitations. Your boss might have discovered, at some point in his past, that some people just don't like him. That realization hurt, but then he discovered an effective fix.

He could fantasize that his team are actually his friends and pretend that everyone loves him, despite his Monday morning tirades. He soon forgets that he was pretending, so now he actually believes that he's very popular. It's easier than tangling with his detractors, easier than doing the work to win people over, and less painful than facing any form of failure or resistance.

Living in the fantasy world allows him to escape from the routine and stress of the day. He might also fear that employees will be de-energized if they face the realities of doing business, such as the fact that the market is down, or that a particular client is impossible. Rather than deal with staff morale issues directly, she may try to lift their spirits into a fantasy world with her.

Unfortunately, when your boss withdraws into the land of make-believe, nothing progressive happens. Innovative ideas may be quashed because everything is already fine and dandy. Conversely, new ideas may be encouraged just for the sake of being creative because they contribute to your TOT's fantasy world.

True TOT Tales

Scrambled TOT at Breakfast

Bosses who live in a fantasy world often project their fantasies onto the entire office. Andy, who works in the quality assurance department for a sports and recreation equipment company in Chicago, had a boss who wanted to be seen as the life of the party. Here's how he used his boss's fantasy to his own advantage.

My boss, Mark, headed the 10-person quality assurance department. For most of us, the work was boring, with lots of record keeping and detail. Because he had a fantasy of becoming a stand-up comic, Mark felt that he had to keep us entertained.

I'm the first to encourage humor in my workday, and Mark did lighten up things a lot. But he repeated the same jokes or at least referred to them several times a week. He was a mediocre joke-teller. Mark had a monotone delivery—he just wasn't that funny. It was embarrassing to listen to him, but he was completely oblivious. He kept on going, even when people winced.

Mark thought his specialty was making puns. Once, a group of us hosted a client breakfast, and my boss had a captive audience. We were all a little nervous when he ordered an omelet because we knew he would go into his standard routine. Sure enough, he spent almost the entire meeting coming up with "clever" puns.

All of us had heard his routine many times before, but he rambled on with his usual material: "eggs-actly," "eggs-traordinary idea," "do you get the yoke," "ignore that egghead, he's really hard-boiled," and so on. The eggs and the jokes were fresh for the client, so we were respectful and laughed even though it was the tenth time we had heard them.

We knew it was important to Mark to be liked by the staff. He occasionally had a bad temper, so we thought it mandatory *to chuckle along. We realized that he abhorred being disliked as much as he wanted to be regarded as an entertainer.*

Because of this trait, whenever we were having difficult conversations with Mark, we used his stand-up fantasy to everyone's benefit. We subtly led him into one of his familiar routines, and we would go along with it. Then we would double back to the business matter at hand, and he saw things in an entirely different, more positive light.

Andy's boss lived in a harmless fantasy world, and once the team understood some of Mark's motivations, they actually encouraged it to keep the peace in the office. Some bosses' fantasies might be a little more disruptive, but as Andy and his coworkers learned, you'll be better poised to cope with your boss when you can figure out why living in La-La Land is a better alternative than reality ... and sometimes, it's better to join him than fight it.

TOT-Taming Tips: Fantasy World

When your child tells you that she's going to build the world's hugest castle with a seesaw for dinosaurs, you smile. You don't smile, however, when your boss tells you he's going to build the world's greatest company by creating some questionable widget that he plans to introduce into the worst market conditions ever.

Unlike kids, corporate execs are supposed to be hard-headed realists. It's disconcerting, to say the least, when your TOT seems to think she's a superhero in spite of glaring evidence to the contrary. Your TOT's fantasies can, in theory, make life more pleasant for you. But when she lives in a dream world that bears no resemblance to the world you inhabit, that's when it's time to implement these tips:

DON'T DO THIS . . .

Assume Everything You Hear Is True. When you accidentally find a consultant behind your boss's closed doors chatting about "rapidly improving efficiencies"—and also notice that half the staff just got laid off—just assume that things are getting highly efficient, rosy, and in good hands, rapidly. Pay no heed to those detractors who call the consultant a hatchet man. Now's the time to ask for a vacation, given the new record level of corporate productivity.

Do This . . .

Separate Fact from Fiction. You need to use your noggin so you can recognize when your boss is exaggerating. This means that you have to do your own homework and stop relying on your boss to interpret events and conditions in the office for you. If you just accept her view or any other worker's view of the world, you might find yourself in a permanent state of Oz. Read company e-mails, industry articles, attend meetings, listen when the Big TOTs speak, and think for yourself.

 DON'T DO THIS . . .

Debunk by Dissing. When your TOT excitedly describes his strategy to make the two-person brokerage office an overnight national franchise sensation, snap your fingers to awaken him out of the stupor. If he thinks you're just groovin' to some faraway beat, stop and try another approach. Roll your eyes in disgust and say, "Boss, this is a sluggish turnaround time, and why doesn't it include the Pacific Rim?!"

Do This ...

Allow Dreamtime. Heck ... it's no picnic being a boss. Give your TOT a break—let her have her fantasies. Like you, she has to deal daily with the fact that she isn't on a cruise to Fiji. Instead, she's in the dreary office next to your drearier cubicle, shuffling papers instead of playing shuffleboard. So play along and be polite. Humor her so that she doesn't bite your head off later when you tell her about your preplanned, five-day trip to Mexico.

 DON'T DO THIS ...

Embrace Martyrdom. Use your boss's delusions as a springboard from which to launch your acting career. Whatever she attributes to you, take as your assignment. Tell her you will work straight through the night, weekend, and even through your mother's appendectomy. Buy yourself a Joan of Arc costume and work on your martyr act. Let it drop that you'd be willing to die for the company and take the competition down in a blaze of glory. If it doesn't get you arrested, it might help make points!

> **Do This ...**
>
> **Let Your TOT See Your Reality.** Even if your boss sees you as a tireless crusader, you need to be able to diplomatically say "no"—or you won't last very long in any job. You can tell her that you respect her dedication, and you sure wish you could help her in the way she wants, but you have other commitments.

TOT-Busters Q&A

Question

My boss thinks I'm a great writer because I once told him that I liked the Romantics. I guess he thought I was referring to romantic poets like Keats and Shelley, but I actually meant I like paperback romantic novels. Now he keeps assigning me to write reports for the company, and he doesn't even review them. He acts as if my writing is flawless. He's not giving me enough input for me to feel that these reports are up to par, based on a couple of e-mailed questions I've received. Should I shatter his illusions? Ask for more input?

Answer

Your writing skills are probably an improvement over what your boss can offer. There's no need to instill a lack of confidence in your abilities.

Here's a case where your TOT's fantasy world can work to your benefit—your career path and reputation. Gently and honestly express your need for a little more input and the benefits it will bring. But do it in a way that is consistent with the pride and excitement that he has for these reports. That said, there's nothing wrong with building on your writing skills with some extra outside training. You'll build more confidence, it will help your career, and who knows, you might even have your own novel under your belt someday!

 Points to Remember

- TOTs retreat into fantasy because reality has thorns.
- TOTs sometimes employ fantasies of a better workplace to keep staff morale high.
- Some TOT fantasizing can work to your benefit.
- Use facts to bring your TOT gently back to reality, but with respect.
- Pay attention to company communications so you don't depend only on your TOT.
- Make sure your TOT respects your own reality and boundaries.

14

Fickleness

About Fickleness

YOU'VE BEEN PLANNING your toddler's birthday for a month. You've been to every store in town, collecting every imaginable party favor related to pirates. You have eye patches, faux swords, and goodie bags stuffed with gold chocolate coins and plastic talking parrots.

Two days before the big day, your toddler wanders into the living room. "Pirates are yucky," he says. "Me wanna robot birt'day." You put the patch over your eye, wave a sword in the air, and say, "Yarrrrrr, matey," trying to re-ignite the earlier buccaneer frenzy. He starts crying. "No! Me hate pirates!!!" he wails, running out of the room.

Cut to your office. You've been working for a month on a series of reports. You have ensured that each report conforms to the content and style agreed on with your boss four weeks

161

ago. Every detail was hashed out in that meeting—from length and style to format and delivery—and you followed instructions to the letter. Finally, you are just minutes from project completion.

While polishing the elements of this enormous undertaking, your indecisive Terrible Office Tyrant (TOT) drops by. Perching casually on the edge of your desk, he says, "You know, a virtual presentation would be more exciting, cutting edge, and cheaper . . . why don't you revise these reports so that they can be delivered online?"

But Why?

Welcome to the world of TOT fickleness. Your boss does not intend to undermine you. In fact, he probably thinks his suggestion is helpful. But you know otherwise: His new brainstorm throws a wrench into a month's worth of hard work—and you go through this scenario almost every time you try to wrap up a project. You plan ahead, you endeavor to be thorough and careful, but over and over, your TOT's capricious suggestions topple your house of cards.

A fickle TOT makes his staff crazy with his inability to make a decision and stick to it. What he likes and dislikes shifts with the wind. One week, he declares he must be copied on all e-mails relating to an initiative. The next week, he insists on brief voicemail updates. And for week three, he wants all communications on the project to occur at the weekly staff meeting.

The only things you can count on if you have a fickle boss are whimsical shifts in priorities and an ongoing state of unreliability. TOTs and toddlers can be just as prone to changing their minds whenever the mood strikes. Look at these similarities:

Fickle Toddler Behavior	Fickle TOT Behavior
Your toddler announces his favorite color is green. He will only wear green from now on. After you scramble to assemble an all-green wardrobe, he declares: "My favorite color is yellow," and will only wear yellow.	Your TOT insists on a suit-and-tie dress code one week, then switches to business casual the next, and then back to suits again, leaving staffers scrambling to adjust their wardrobes.
He demands the latest piece of overpriced plastic from the toy store. He whines for days, "Can I have Face Punchin' Pete?! Pleeeeaaaase!" Once you cave in, he becomes giddy with glee for 60 seconds and then discards ol' Pete under the bed, where it sits untouched for a generation.	He demands that the department spend the entire tech budget on new software. He stomps around for days, telling everyone "This technology is mission critical!" When the software is purchased, he finds it too difficult to use and immediately loses interest. The software package now props open the break room door.
Your toddler begs to be taken to the latest movie starring Grimly the Great Gorilla. Whenever a commercial airs, she squeals, "Love Grimly, want to see Grimly!" So you take her. Five minutes after the movie begins, she gets bored and demands to be taken home.	Your TOT unexpectedly pulls your team off projects to attend a trade show. When the team returns to the office, the boss has no interest in hearing about the show's results. Instead, he whines that too many projects were left unfinished.
On Monday, your toddler says Jim is his best friend. Tuesday, it's Sam. Wednesday, it's David. Thursday . . .	On Monday, your TOT says Anne is the department's top performer. Tuesday, it's Ellen. Wednesday, it's Martha. Thursday . . .

What causes fickle behavior? In your toddler, fickle behavior is the result of an undeveloped decision-making system. The still-growing brain may have mastered the art of speaking, shouting, and even giving orders. But it has not yet developed to the point that it can consistently choose a direction and stick with it.

Sadly, many make it to adulthood—even the executive suite—still lacking these critical decision-making skills. Your boss is not two years old. So what makes her act this way?

Where Does Fickleness Come From?

Often, fickle behavior is motivated by fear. Your TOT boss is afraid of being stuck with a bad decision. To ensure that never happens, her priorities, policies, and actions are in constant flux, so that she can rarely be pinned down to any one choice.

In a world where executives are routinely hammered for being too entrenched in one approach, this utter lack of commitment can actually be a way to get ahead. Who can blame your TOT for a failed project—if she never formally supported it? If it tanks, her constant shifting will make it easy for her to "prove" that she was against it. Worse yet, this dodging can make you the scapegoat if you stuck your neck out to promote the idea.

Fickle behavior can also be brought on by lack of planning. If your boss is the type who operates without a long-term strategic plan, she will be susceptible to the lure of the latest thing.

Finally, fickleness is driven by the classic syndrome of buyer's remorse. An insecure TOT boss will be fickle because she can't convince herself her last decision was any good.

Many Forms of Fickle

Fickleness can take many shapes, none of which are particularly enjoyable to experience. Fortunately, there are ways to finesse fickle bosses.

Lack of Backbone

Your TOT boss repeatedly changes direction out of fear of being tagged as unimaginative, or worse, wrong. It could be that he lacks confidence in his decision-making practices. In that case, your job is to subtly help shore up his ability to pick the right idea and stay the course. This may entail providing him with additional research, lining up support from others, or demonstrating how he's following in the footsteps of other successful managers. The key: Make your TOT feel safe, and he will be less likely to flip-flop.

Missing Road Map

Any decision today looks fine because your TOT is operating without an overall strategy. That means anyone who is whispering in her ear on any given day may get her to make a decision. Should a new staffer gain her attention tomorrow, watch for that decision to be overruled. You might volunteer to help develop a departmental plan. Although it's a massive task, it could pay off in the long run.

Spinning Wheels

Some bosses simply do not know when to move on. A decision has been made, but these fickle TOTs must circle back again and again, searching for the right answer, driving everyone crazy with their inability to choose a course of action.

In some cases, these bosses know what to do, but they're afraid to make a move because it might hurt feelings or ruffle feathers. These TOTs need your support to take a strong leadership stand, which you can do by bolstering them.

Option Overload

You may be enabling your TOT's fickle behavior by offering too many choices. Like a toddler in a toy store, your TOT may be

immobilized by the vast possibilities. For these bosses, fewer
choices are best to mitigate the deer-in-the-headlights syndrome.

- -

True TOT Tales

What's for Dinner?

Marcos is the director of marketing for an e-commerce firm. He works
for a senior vice president—known throughout the organization for her
indecisive management style.

It was nearing the holiday season, and my boss was in a
quandary: she could not decide how to celebrate the season. She
was stuck for weeks between recommending that employees all
receive turkeys or be taken out for dinner and drinks. The
back-and-forth was giving us all whiplash.

We were all trapped in her fickle behavior. And although it
didn't really matter which way she went, her indecision was
wasting valuable time and mental energy.

The boss frequently sought our input on her predicament. It
seems we were taking a show-of-hands vote on the topic every
three days. And no matter which way the wind blew, she found
a way to make a decision—and then deviate from it. It seemed
the turkey/dinner debate would never end.

It was clear as the weeks wore on that the boss's biggest
concern was that she would finally make a decision on this topic
and that it would somehow be the "wrong" call.

Finally, in an attempt to stop the constant chatter on the
topic, I took a more dedicated research approach. I polled the
staff and created a written document, analyzing the pros and
cons of each holiday meal option.

Faced with actual research in written form, my boss was
finally able to make a decision: turkey. And then anytime she

waffled or wavered, we only needed to guide her back to the rock-solid research foundation. That kept her—finally—locked in place.

I learned a lot from this experience. To help my boss overcome her fickle tendencies, she needs a foundation of objective research. Without it, any decision she makes is subject to change—and change again!

Marcos knew the madness was literally gobbling up too much time. He took control of the situation and found a framework that tamed his boss's fickle behavior. Marcos generated written documentation on the projects, and encouraged his boss to make a decision based on it. When his boss wavered, Marcos reached for his new secret weapon—documentation—to fend off the once-inevitable change of heart.

TOT-Taming Tips: Fickleness

Although your TOT's fickle behavior may drive you to distraction, there are many ways you can blunt the impact of this trait. Just as toddlers are able to overcome this behavior with steady guidance, a fickle TOT can be managed in the direction of more rational, consistent decisions.

 DON'T DO THIS . . .

Out-Fickle the Boss. Cut in front of your boss on the cafeteria line. Walk back and forth repeatedly in front of the counter, gazing at the sandwiches, and ask your TOT: "Which should I order—the tuna or the egg salad?" When he recommends the egg salad, say "Oh, but my cholesterol is 280. I can't have eggs. Should I go for the tuna?" When he says, "Sure, order the tuna," say "Oh, but the mercury content in tuna is terrible." Decline each recommendation down the menu, citing the killer ingredients in each one.

Do This . . .

Follow a Procedure. Your fickle TOT needs a plan of action. Set up a process by which decisions are made and encourage everyone to follow them to the letter. A little rigorous structure and follow-through will help your boss with a direct plan of action.

 DON'T DO THIS . . .

Jump on Each Edict. Take every word your boss utters as an immediate call to action. If he suggests looking into e-commerce, drop everything else until you've become a national guru on the subject. If he comments on a good move by the competition, run over there in disguise and deliver donuts to get some valuable market intelligence. If he says there must be better documentation, document it!

Do This . . .

Listen for Cues. Sometimes your TOT will waver on an issue when she really does have a position, but wants to empower you. You have to be practically a mind reader to catch this, but if you miss the signals, you could go off into outer space with a direction that's misguided. Major clues include statements such as: "I'll leave it up to you then," or "If you really want to go that way, let's do it," or, after a lengthy discussion, "You decide." All of them require you to take the cue and then delve further with questions, rather than having that mixed feeling when you leave a meeting.

 DON'T DO THIS …

Suggest a Million Paths. Assume that your boss waffles because he just doesn't have good options to choose from. When it's time to hire a new office manager, bring him every resume—all 1,589 of them. If he asks you to narrow the field, divide the resumes into two piles—one-page resumes on the left and multipagers on the right, and see what he thinks.

Do This …

Cull the Herd. The best way to get your fickle boss to make a decision is to reduce the number of choices before they come to him. This way, it will be easier for him to see the right path forward. A young child may be stymied by all the choices in a restaurant, but she will be able to make a choice when provided with a special kids menu. Make the same first cut for your fickle TOT or consider presenting only the best choice, and everyone will breathe easier.

DON'T DO THIS . . .

Bicker. Be ready to fight whenever the boss starts to speak. If he says, "I've changed my mind about keeping office décor understated in that dull, oak motif. I want to inspire creativity with neon lights and open spaces," roll your eyes and huff. "Nobody wants that, and anyway, I've just ordered an understated desk blotter to match my oak desk." Say no to every change until your TOT is exhausted.

Do This . . .

Pick Your Battles. Not every battle is worth the fallout. Be sure that when you decide to argue with your boss, the reasons are valid. If your boss has chosen to shift the venue of a client meeting, will that really undermine the outcome? A lack of commitment to the staff may require more diplomatic questioning on your part.

TOT-Busters Q&A

Question

My boss contradicts herself almost daily. The most obvious infraction is that she can't decide who to assign to a project. Invariably, one of us will start a project, and several others will pick it up along the way, as she changes her mind. Ultimately, we step on each other's toes. Should we just say, "Pick a path and stick with it?"

Answer

It's tempting, but with TOTs, like toddlers, you must gently encourage them in one direction or another. It's best to determine what the TOT really needs in advance of a project. She may not know herself because she hasn't developed this skill fully yet and is in action mode without a strategy. She might even appreciate your efforts. For example, you might ask questions like, "What range of skills will the project need from start to finish?" or "Should we set up a committee?" Milder inquiries will work better than a blunt one with a fickle boss.

 Points to Remember

Just like a toddler, a fickle TOT may want to change his or her behavior, but needs help along the way. Consider these approaches:

- Reduce choices.
- Present research.
- Pick your battles.
- Don't condone or mimic fickle behavior.
- Listen for hidden cues.
- Provide a path.

15

Helplessness

About Helplessness

YOU ARE WORKING at a rapidly expanding company for a dynamic, highly successful boss—a sales and marketing whiz who is at the top of her game. Your boss's drive and motivation is well known, which is the reason you were originally attracted to the position. But after a few months on the job, you've noticed that the brilliant wheeler-dealer is something of a Terrible Office Tyrant (TOT).

You've observed that she has the need for certain security blankets when she strays outside her comfort zone of schmoozing clients in person. For example, since the last computer upgrade two months ago, your TOT has been calling on you (and not her admin) to help her send out e-mail blasts. At first, she said she was too busy, and you agreed to help. After the third blast, you realized you had moved from simply sending her e-mails to editing them first—and now, you have ended up writing, editing, and sending them.

You notice other tell-tale signs. She asks you to take all notes during client conference calls, and after each major point, she asks you if you got that down. Later on, she can't find the "most salient" point made in the notes you e-mailed her, and calls you in a panic to ask for a quick recap.

The way she fumbled for that simple information made you wonder if she wasn't able to open her e-mail or the file at all. Come to think of it, she always carries a huge stack of paper around and has never responded to a text message. "Yikes," you think, "my boss borders on tech illiteracy."

Something about the word "new" virtually morphs her into a three-year-old on her first day at preschool. When the teacher says, "We're playing a game. Come join us," your toddler hides behind you and says, "I don't know how." If you arm some TOTs with the latest cell phone or wireless device, hardware or software, they are just as helpless.

But Why?

Like a dependent toddler who finds it easier and safer to engage a parent in every unfamiliar or complicated activity, your TOT relies on you to get him through many daily challenges. And, like a child who is told, "Brush your own teeth; you are a big boy," your TOT may not respond kindly to: "Do it yourself."

Technology is a huge contributor to helplessness. Of course, there are a number of other major factors that turn big bad TOTs into little lost tykes. New management personnel or policies can easily freak out a TOT. Big changes with clients and competitors can knock a TOT out of her comfort zone, too. And, it can be something as simple as reorganizing the office. ("Where are they keeping the pens now? Agh!")

"I'd Rather Have You Do It"

Helpless bosses can also be sneaky bosses. If they know someone else can perform the task, it's easier to never master it—and to always have an employee do the heavy lifting.

Everyone likes to be needed. But your boss seems to call you before he makes an effort to solve a problem. You may feel trapped by your own competence because when your TOT looks bad, to some degree, you look bad. When he has trouble setting up a videoconference, neither of you want the other department heads rolling their eyes and muttering about the "caveman" down the hall.

Your TOT is often embarrassed by the void in his skill set, but not so much that he wants to overcome it. As long as you are there, he has a safety net. Like a toddler joining a new playgroup, he gets anxious. His dependence may be flattering, but the time you spend TOT-sitting could cost you and the company productivity. You may feel like you are playing the role of parent at work, and after you review the parallels between TOTs and toddlers, you'll see that you aren't too far from the truth.

Helpless Toddler Behavior	Helpless TOT Behavior
You put all the items your child needs to take to preschool on his bed and show him how to put them in his backpack. Then you say, "Now you try it." He throws a fit, screaming, "It's too hard! You do it!"	Your boss has to go to a meeting in New York. You set up a trial run of the stellar presentation you've been putting together for the past month. She gets through two slides and gives up, "I can't do it. I'm sending you to New York instead."
As soon as she sits down with her homework, she says she doesn't understand what to do. You explain the first problem and she comprehends it. But when you try to get her to do the next one on her own, she moans, "I can't do it. I don't know how. Show me."	As soon as your boss starts to work on the quality assurance report, he asks for your help. You show him the ropes, but when you get up to leave, he says, "I need this now and I don't have time to learn all these programs."

Helpless Toddler Behavior	Helpless TOT Behavior
You ask your child to feed the dog, which he had promised to do earlier. He says, "I don't want to. I hate that stinky dog food." You say, "Okay, I guess Buster is out of luck. We'll have to give him to a little boy who will take care of him." Buster looks at you and starts howling. You feed Buster.	You remind your boss that the big client meeting is today and that he needs to have his presentation set up in an hour. He says, "I hate putting those slides together. I'm going to wing it." At the meeting, the client tries to bite her lip during your boss's embarrassing missteps. You help out.
You hear banging and crashing in her bedroom followed by crying. She was supposed to be getting dressed to go to Aunt Mary's. You walk in and she is under the covers. "My socks are turned around. They're lumpy on top!"	You hear banging and crashing from the corner office followed by swearing. Your boss's new flat-screen monitor is on the floor in several pieces. "I thought it was one of those touch-screens . . . and it wouldn't work."

If you're the exasperated helpmate of a helpless TOT, you probably have something to do with it. You may have generously extended yourself one time too many, and now your boss just throws up her hands whenever she sees a "Server Error" message pop up. Instead of working it out, she calls or texts you: "Help . . . my computer. Can you come over?"

At least with little kids, you know that helping them usually leads to a burst of independence and pride in accomplishing a new skill. If you don't encourage children to try things on their own and deal with failure, they can stay helpless—or at least dependent—forever. A good parent encourages the child to step up. With a TOT, it's a little harder to navigate.

There's no point arguing with a helpless TOT. At this point, you may not know if it is laziness or force of habit that keeps her so reliant on you for things, no matter how small, that she can't seem to master.

If you fight back, chances are your TOT is going to pull rank on you. There is a fine line between being a "good" person and being a "gullible" person. You don't want to see your boss fail, but you also are not responsible for her success. Make sure you haven't unwittingly become an "enabler." A change in the way you operate could result in a big change in your boss's ability to deal with her own daily challenges. (By the way, helplessness is often related to neediness, so check out Chapter 19 on that TOT trait, too.)

True TOT Tales

The Case of Phone-O-Phobia

Larry's boss had a fear of telephone technology, which took up a lot of Larry's time, and it soon began draining him. Here's what happened.

My boss, Marie, is a classic technophobe, but in her case, it's the telephone, not computer, that has her stressed out. I guess she's embarrassed about this because she gets me to help her secretly. I mean, I'm a graphic designer. Business telephones just seem pretty easy.

Anyway, she went crazy when the new phone system was installed; she had barely mastered the old one. To me, it seems normal for people to get confused by computers. But telephones seem so basic. She was dragging me into her office a few times every day to help with three-way calling, remote messaging, voicemail, or other features.

Then, we got an e-mail about a class being offered by the company that installed the phone system. Apparently, other people also had difficulty with the new features and asked for some instruction. This seemed like the perfect solution, so I *suggested to Marie that she sign up for the class. She said she would, but on the day of class, she blew it off.*

I was really disappointed by this. I told her I was going to ask our IT person to come see her and basically repeat the class for her privately. She refused and said that she was too embarrassed to let anyone know about her problem—except me. It was "our little secret."

Despite the special place I held as her confidant, I realized things had gone too far. I needed to communicate my position clearly. I scheduled a meeting so I could explain why I needed to set some boundaries. I told her that my regular work was suffering from the constant troubleshooting. I diplomatically made a recommendation about the limited amount of time I could dedicate to teaching her the phone basics. Essentially, I was politely cutting her off.

When the phone trainer came back the following week to teach a class for those people who missed the first one, I was pleased to see that my boss attended. I've only gotten one call from her, and that was when she really was in a crisis and didn't have time to read the manual beforehand.

I learned that there are ways to distance yourself from a helpless boss without damaging your relationship. Everybody has weaknesses, and everyone needs help sometime—just not every time.

By offering to help with the phone system, Larry realized he had unwittingly enabled his boss to be helpless. Larry needed to let Marie know that he was being pulled away from his core responsibilities. After all, Marie had hired him to do design work, and if that work was behind schedule, it was going to affect both of them. Marie just needed the wake-up call to see how her helplessness had turned into a distraction.

TOT-Taming Tips: Helplessness

There are many ways to deal with a helpless boss and turn the problem into a positive experience. And, there are ways to make things worse. Here are a few tips:

 DON'T DO THIS ...

Troubleshoot Full-Time. Walk right into your TOT's office first thing, and without even saying "Good morning," start out with "Okay, What's the problem?" You know there's going to be one, so let's get to it. "Do you need me to open an attachment? Install software? You name it." Your boss will appreciate your "can-do" attitude, and you can hang out there most of the day.

Do This ...

Suggest Alternatives. Be honest about what you do and don't know. Offer to find the person who does know. If your TOT needs computer assistance, offer to call the IT person. If her anxiety is about her ability to take good notes during a meeting, suggest taking a tape recorder. Don't lie about your expertise, but if you're a novice, don't spend a lot of time figuring out what your boss should do. Find a way for both of you to become more independent.

 DON'T DO THIS ...

Groan and Moan Publicly. It helps if everyone, including your TOT, knows how much you do for her—and how much you suffer. When she asks you to move her convertible into the shade because her time works out to $14,700 per hour, scream as if all your internal organs were suddenly removed. Leave her office rolling on the floor toward the elevator, yelling, "Why me? Why me?"

Do This . . .

Draw the Line. Have boundaries and stand your ground. If you've let your boss get away with helplessness for a long time, it's going to be difficult to break old habits. With a child, you know that unless he learns to tie his own shoes, he'll be in a world of trouble when he starts interacting with his peers. Similarly, your boss needs to be weaned off his dependency on you or he'll embarrass himself. Plus, you'll never live to see another vacation day if you respond to every request.

 DON'T DO THIS . . .

Broadcast His Helplessness. If your TOT calls you from his car because he is lost and too embarrassed to tell anyone, say, "No problem. I'll put you on speaker phone and see if our team of experts can gather for an emergency pow-wow and guide you—hold on." By the time he envisions the entire department convening to hear the details of his latest odyssey, he'll hang up in a nanosecond.

> **Do This ...**
>
> **Have a Word in Private.** A helpless TOT may admit to needing something, but she will never volunteer the fact that she is totally clueless. If you can privately convey to your boss—without being preachy or negative—that you understand that she needs your help, but that you are trying to tackle your regular workload, you can help break the dependency cycle. You'd be surprised at how often a TOT doesn't realize she's being needy to the point of distraction.

TOT-Busters Q&A

Question

I'm a supervisor at an insurance company, and my boss keeps asking me to handle tasks that are administrative (and sometimes personal) in nature. I don't think she realizes how much of my time is taken by these requests. For example, she often asks me for the names of hot new restaurants because her admin doesn't dine out much, and I seem so "cosmopolitan." I gave her some ideas, and got her a few more online, but how can I get her to handle her personal tasks without alienating her?

Answer

Try mentioning that you'll get to her request as soon as you complete the important business project she assigned you earlier. After hearing this response enough times, she'll likely see that you are trying to stay focused on work for her own benefit. Hopefully, she'll think twice before asking for tips about the hippest cafes nearby. If you have time, though, you might volunteer suggestions if you had a great meal somewhere.

 ## Points to Remember

- Don't get trapped by your own expertise. Encourage your boss to learn by doing.
- Assume the best-case scenario—your TOT wants the situation to improve. Find ways to take the training wheels off over the long term, instead of repeatedly fixing the same issue.
- Set boundaries and stick to them.
- Suggest positive solutions. Be creative. Look for training solutions or other specialists who can help your TOT without getting yourself trapped in the "resident expert" box.
- Stop enabling. You may be half of the problem if you are the type of person who needs to be needed.

16

Irrational Fears

About Irrational Fears

You've been called to a big meeting with your Terrible Office Tyrant (TOT) and some key vendors. You honestly are not sure what to expect, given some of the paranoid behavior your TOT has exhibited in recent meetings.

It began with a simple, but unusual, request. Your TOT insisted on having several layers of staff present at the January vendor meeting. He said he wanted everyone present to witness what ideas were being put forth to the vendors as a "precaution."

Then, right before the February vendor meeting, it escalated. Your boss asked you unexpectedly if "we've made sure we have a 'documenter' before we start today's vendor meeting, you know, as a defensive measure?" You scrambled to round up an extra staffer to take notes, but everything worked out.

However, today, the paranoia seems to be getting worse and this time, the irrational requests are centered on the meeting with the company's biggest supplier. Although you've already lined up

183

his "documenter" and even have a paralegal on call, he now has asked you to invite all 12 staff members to today's meeting. "We need lots of witnesses to make sure they don't steal our secrets and give them to our competitor next week."

In this age of lawsuit mania and intellectual property theft, it's natural to be a little on edge about potential litigation. But this scaredy-cat boss has taken it to new unimagined levels. He lives in constant fear of getting ripped off and double-crossed.

But Why?

Everyone has fears of some kind. But TOTs can take these self-manufactured, illogical anxieties and virtually will them into reality, affecting everyone in sight. Even though they represent little more than creepy shadows on the wall for a toddler lying in bed, this fear is just as real to your TOT.

Irrational fears are commonplace in childhood. All of us can remember a time when something perfectly harmless, such as a room full of unfamiliar people or a dark hallway, seemed insurmountably scary. Toddlers, without the life experience to process some of these unfamiliar events, can react to them with horror.

TOTs, despite their more advanced age, are susceptible to the very same fears. An experience that most people find utterly unremarkable is one that can send your boss into a spiraling tizzy of TOT terror.

Fearful TOTs can be quite dangerous to business. While toddlers who are incapable of calming themselves during this emotional overload may do some damage while acting out, paranoid TOTs actually have the power and ability to drag down an entire organization with them during a corner-office conniption.

Nonsensical fears can manifest themselves in the behavior of your tyke at home or your boss in the office.

Irrational Toddler Behavior	**Irrational TOT Behavior**
Your toddler fears water and won't set foot in the tub. She stands by the tub filled with bubbles and toys, wailing, "No no no! I won't go in! Sharks will eat me! I'll slide down the drain!"	Your boss fears presentations and refuses to set foot in the conference room filled with potential clients and frets, "My pitch isn't ready. They'll hate it. They've already decided to go with a competitor. I'll flop and my reputation will be ruined!"
He worries that "stepping on cracks will break his mother's back" and refuses to walk in a straight line down the sidewalk, bobbing and weaving. In this effort to "save mom," her shoulder is practically dislocated from the tugs and pulls.	She worries she's getting fired, when she hears Super TOT is making a visit next week to her department. In advance of the meeting, she takes drastic action, reshuffling department assignments and replacing long-standing procedures with new, complicated policies.
She refuses to go to preschool. "I'll have no friends. Nobody will play with me. I'll be all alone."	He refuses to attend industry functions. "What if no one at the cocktail party wants to talk to me? What can I say, anyway?"
Afraid of being alone, he trails his father through the house, clutches his hand, clothes, and leg, refusing under any circumstance to be left solo in any room.	Afraid of being alone, she trails employees into their offices, the conference room, and the break room. When forced to return to her own office, she regularly summons you.

Irrational fears are common during childhood because it is often an insecure time—a period in life when one is not in control of one's destiny. Adults and their mysterious ways seem to rule the planet and little people are left to scurry along to keep up.

That's enough to make a child worry that shadows on the wall or noises in the basement might actually be something truly dangerous. After all, many things are unexplained. It takes life experience to sort out the scary from the dangerous.

For your TOT, irrational fears are often reinventions of past insecurities. Once again, fear and uncertainty surface and manifest themselves in irrational responses instead of logical concerns.

Fear Comes from Everywhere! Look out!

Irrational fears come from a variety of sources.

Shyness

Your TOT may be bashful and this may result in a host of irrational fears, from refusing to address the staff to avoiding industry meetings to virtually hiding under the desk when visitors arrive.

Insecurity

A twist on the shy boss syndrome, the insecure TOT is not certain where she fits in. She may have been recently promoted. So, should she behave like one of the gang . . . or one of the bosses? This insecurity may result in irrational fears such as "transitional break room phobia": "should I sit with my friends—or with the my new peer managers?"

Lack of Ability

Like a toddler who runs away from a tricycle, your TOT may display what seem to be irrational fears because of a true lack of skills. Is he really afraid of the new software? Or does he just have no clue how to use it?

Self-Preservation

Let's face it, in today's business world, paranoia is practically a virtue. Bosses who are constantly on high alert, with one eye in the rear view mirror, are the most likely to survive—even if they drive their teams crazy in the process. If your TOT shows an irrational fear of getting fired, it may make you nuts, but it's self-preservation in action. And remember, it may stem from Super TOT's inexplicable anxiety over company failure, which always trickles down.

True TOT Tales

A Fear of Short-Sleeves

Chris, a section manager at an IT services firm, unwittingly triggered one of his boss's irrational fears. He thought they were having a relatively straightforward conversation, but he was unaware that his TOT boss actually saw "monsters" lurking everywhere.

> We're a technical services firm and most of our employees (self-proclaimed geeks) have limited contact with customers. No one visits our department of 25. Our conference room is so under-used that the interns store their bikes in it.
>
> So, I approached my boss about letting my group go "business casual." After all, clients relied on the technical expertise of my staff. They didn't need to know what the techies were wearing in-house when they saved clients from IT disasters.
>
> In a long face-to-face meeting with my boss, he agreed this would be a reasonable move and said we really should get a memo out—under his name. As we finished up, he said to me, "Let's move forward with it."

And so I did. I drew up a memo, and assuming this meeting was my green light, I sent it out to my division under his name. My boss freaked out. He reacted as if I had let a cobra loose in the executive bathroom. He shrieked about how I had doomed us both by prematurely announcing the program.

*Apparently, "move forward" meant "draft a memo." He was sure he'd be fired instantly, and wouldn't even take his boss's call the next morning. Turns out, she was calling to congratulate him. When she couldn't get him on the phone, she eventually stopped by and found him cowering in his office.
"What a great idea. It's just the morale boost the department needed. I'm so glad you're on top of this!"*

In a heartbeat, my boss's mood flipped 180 degrees. He was jovial, complimentary, and even took a victory lap around the department. After that incident, I made sure to check in more carefully before taking proactive steps. I also tried to become the "voice of reason" when he was excessively worried. Over time, I think my calmness was contagious.

Chris learned a valuable lesson about irrational fears in TOT bosses: they come and go with lightning speed. From that point forward, Chris learned that moving with calm, deliberate steps was the key to keeping his boss on an even keel. That way, he could mitigate actions that might set off his TOT's illogical anxieties.

TOT-Taming Tips: Irrational Fears

The key to managing irrational fears in your TOT boss is knowing the triggers. Staying ahead of things that set her off will help you avoid the fit that ensues when she feels afraid or insecure. Think of it as investing in a night-light. It's a small step to take to ensure your TOT boss will not wake up screaming in the middle of the night. These TOT-Taming Tips will help keep you off Nightmare Island.

 DON'T DO THIS …

Stoke Anxiety. On a daily basis, tell your TOT that Big TOT seems to favor Jones, a rival department head, "because he seems really dedicated." Then, ask your boss, "Don't you think Jones should get some recognition for all the revenue he's brought in, and for all his great leadership skills? Don't you think he deserves the Manager of the Year award, two weeks in Barbados, or at least a promotion?"

Do This …

Stroke His Ego. Focus on your boss's mental outlook. Avoid talking about issues that provoke fear by keeping things positive, and be careful not to flatter other managers often. Keep handy a short list of your TOT's successes and comments that you've heard about her from other TOTs, including Super TOT, so you can sing her praises on short notice. For example, when your TOT begins to fret that her boss likes another manager best, be set to jump in with, "Sure, but that manager never developed a plan like yours that saved the company hundreds of thousands of dollars."

 DON'T DO THIS …

Send Out Breaking News. If you work for a public company, and your company's stock is taking a nosedive, send your boss (and all the bosses up the chain) e-mail or text updates on the latest drop in price—and any sell recommendations by industry analysts. Don't obsess over separating fact from rumor. Information is information. Label subject headings with words such as "Wow!" and "Unbelievable!" Don't forget to include the board of directors in your updates.

Do This . . .

Be Fair and Balanced. Snippets of data may only make your TOT nervous. Wait until a broader picture emerges. Be sure you can answer the question, "What does this mean?" before sending any information the boss's way. Uncertainty breeds irrational fears. If your TOT asks about a still-forming trend, tell him you're watching the situation: "Actually there's not enough data on this yet to make a clear call. I'm on it and will get back to you as soon as the picture clears."

 DON'T DO THIS . . .

Fly the Red Flags. Your company is riding on the success of its core product introduced a year ago and your TOT is still receiving accolades for his vision in bringing the product to market. Share your theory throughout the office on how "two kids with a Wi-Fi connection and some silicon chips" could start selling the same product in six weeks. Then, drop by your TOT's office and tell him you thought you saw a couple of high school geeks with laptops and lab coats hanging around the parking lot with your closest competitor. Then exit, leaving your TOT to ponder the possibilities.

Do This ...

Stay in the Present. Deal with reality, not possibilities. When your TOT begins to speculate about bad things that may happen sometime in the future, remind her that none of it has happened. Prepare deflective humor to use when the boss launches into the "What If?" riff.

 DON'T DO THIS ...

Strike Fear via the Suggestion Box. At the next staff meeting, bring up your recent suggestion to the home office that employees conduct performance reviews of their bosses in front of the entire staff. Mention that this approach has never been taken before and shows out-of-the-suggestion-box thinking.

Do This ...

Prepare, Prepare, Prepare. Know in advance what your boss is afraid of. Is it being fired? Exposed? Ridiculed? Understanding the core triggers will help you prepare for outbursts of irrationality that may be coming downstream. If new competitive information sets your boss on high alert, stay aware of marketplace threats. Provide your TOT with written plans and clear next steps in advance of meetings, so that he won't have the opportunity to panic.

TOT-Busters Q&A

Question

My boss is in a constant state of alarm over the health of our company. He's always on the lookout for signs of impending disaster. He's subscribed to every possible online newsfeed and he sends alerts out to all of us. Last week, when a competitor was sued, my boss acted as if this had happened to us. He called an emergency meeting to discuss the issue, insisting we drop everything and draft an emergency response plan. Now I'm getting fearful that I'll become more like my boss.

Answer

Panic grows in a vacuum. The key to managing your boss's irrational fear of corporate collapse is to continuously provide him with information that makes him feel safe and secure. That may be market reports indicating the success of one of your products or productivity charts that show how well he's managing his staff. You can't control what goes on out in the wider industry—and neither can he. But you can help him focus on areas of positive development that may lessen his unfounded worry.

 Points to Remember

- To tame a TOT's irrational fears:
  - Go slowly.
  - Shower him with useful facts and information.

- – Avoid sarcasm, joking around or pranks, or anything that might be misinterpreted.
- – Don't take it personally.
- Be the voice of reason.
- Irrational fears are often manifestations of deep insecurities. Understanding the underpinnings will help you preempt corporate panic attacks.
- Even when your TOT boss is in the throes of unreasonable anxiety, keep in mind that these fears are often fleeting. Wait for the funnel cloud to move on and try not to get sucked in.

17

Forgetfulness

About Forgetfulness

YOU'VE JUST WALKED into your office after spending an hour in horrible traffic, after dropping off your Terrible Office Tyrant (TOT) at the airport. All you've done the last few days is help him prepare for his big meeting at corporate headquarters. But, it will all be worth it when he presents the proposal you created and hands out the report you spent hours formatting and proofing.

You stayed up until midnight setting up all the materials he needs. You placed them on his office chair, so he wouldn't forget anything. Finally, you can focus on the rest of your agenda: creating the departmental standards manual for your employees. You put your feet up and look forward to a few days without having to be a caretaker.

Just as your feet hit the desktop, the phone rings. Uh-oh. Caller ID says your TOT's on the line. "Hi, boss!"

"Thank God you're there. I think I really screwed up." Uh-oh . . . again.

"You got me to the airport so early, I figured I had time to get a drink, so I went to the bar and ordered a Bloody Mary . . . to relax. The next thing I knew they were calling final boarding for my plane, so I ran to the gate and just made it on the flight."

"So, what's the problem?"

"Umm. I think I left my briefcase in the bar. I can't remember which hotel I'm supposed to go to. And now I can't find that little memory flash stick thingy that you put the presentation on. What the heck should I do?"

"Sheesh," you think to yourself, "he's like a little kid. He almost 'missed the bus,' he 'forgot his lunchbox,' and if he ever lost his cell phone . . . ! How can someone with so much responsibility need me as a surrogate parent?"

But Why?

A scatterbrained TOT is reminiscent of a child so involved in momentary distractions that he can't keep track of his belongings, or where he is supposed to be, or many other matters related to job survival. This may be tolerable in a three-year-old, but it can be downright alarming in a fifty-year-old.

Are there any benefits to having a forgetful TOT? Take heart, there are. The silver lining is that she won't remember your mistakes any more than she will remember her own. You will have more freedom to excel and work independently. Similarly, you are more likely to win arguments because she won't have all the facts straight. If you remind her, "You asked me never to cc: Harrison," she'll likely be aware of her memory lapses and back off.

Let's examine more closely how both toddlers and bosses share this challenge.

Forgetful Toddler Behavior	Forgetful TOT Behavior
In the rush to make the school bus, your child forgets his lunchbox and tells the teacher, "Mommy didn't make lunch for me today."	In the rush to make her flight, your TOT forgets her report notes and tells the division head, "My assistant didn't finish my report on time."
You remind your toddler to hold on to her dolly at the supermarket, or she won't be able to bring it again. Minutes later, she wails, "Mommy! Where's my dolly?"	You remind your boss about his 2:00 PM meeting several times. At 2:15 PM, he runs past your office screaming, "Why didn't you remind me about this meeting? I'm late!"
When you turn off the television, she goes ballistic. "No! I hate you, Daddy." But as soon as you bring in a plate of cookies, she perks up, forgetting her rant, and says, "I love you, Daddy."	Your boss is upset that you cut her off in a meeting and won't talk to you all day. The next morning, when you bring in donuts for the team, she smiles, forgetting yesterday's blow-up.
Your son begs to help you make dinner every night, and so you finally allow him to help make cheese sandwiches. But he doesn't show up when called. You find him in the backyard making mud pies. He tells you, "I made other food."	You've been working 24/7 and your boss decides to reward you. "I'll take you to lunch tomorrow at Bistro-Trendy." You get dressed up the next day and start looking forward to a great meal. At lunchtime, she says, "Can you cover the phones? I'm gonna grab a bite with Helen."

There are many reasons why people forget things, ranging from mild to serious. If you have a forgetful boss, your first strategy should be to figure out what's wrong. Is she generally pleasant, but sometimes preoccupied or distracted? Does he seem like he's juggling so many balls that he just doesn't have time to attend to every detail?

On the other hand, you may notice that your boss's forgetfulness is linked to specific behaviors or situations. For example, in the morning he's focused and productive, but after lunch, he can't seem to stay on track. You might be seeing a caffeine or sugar slump—or someone who just runs out of steam in the afternoon.

Insufficient Memory Alert!

The most common cause of TOT forgetfulness is that your boss suffers the same affliction as the average toddler: he is easily distracted by the next new thing and skips over details—like where he parked his car, or that group reports are due every Monday.

With some TOTs, absent-mindedness is indicative of a "big picture" thinker. He has his eye on the big prize, but he tends to overlook the small stuff—that's for you to handle. Other TOTs may use forgetfulness as an excuse to get out of doing things they dislike doing.

Using you to take care of details is one thing, but blaming you for her errors is another. If your boss is absentminded and makes costly errors that are reflected in the company's bottom line, you should attempt to rein in that behavior.

Try to encourage personal responsibility in your boss, without nagging or lecturing. As with toddlers, positive reinforcement goes a long way.

True TOT Tales

A Glass Half Full

Tanya was a merchandise assistant who had recently started a new job where she wanted to express her creativity and demonstrate her administrative skills. But she hit a snag with her first assignment.

I started working for a home décor company. My task was to find glass containers within a tight budget, for flowering plants my boss was buying for an upcoming trade show. I was really excited to show her what I could do. I spent the day driving all over town visiting discount stores. I found some really unusual glass candy jars at rock-bottom prices. At the end of the day, I brought them into the office, thinking I had found the perfect choices.

My boss first glared at her watch, then at me. Then as I took out my "gems," she screeched, "Yaaaargh! These will detract from the plants I bought! Just go to the supermarket like I told you, and bring back some unobtrusive glass food jars!"

I was dumbfounded. I dashed over to a grocery store and brought food jars to the office. Later, I reviewed her e-mail. It was vague, reading: "glass jars in different sizes," with no specific instructions. I asked her how I could avoid this kind of a problem in the future. She said, "I'm a busy person. I can't put everything in an e-mail. Take better notes." As frustrating as that statement was, it taught me a lesson.

From that moment on, I followed up on her e-mails with an e-mail of my own, restating my task. She began to realize just how vague her requests were, and began investing a little more time upfront. She started to make lists more often and would then carefully communicate to me, in writing. (My boss probably noticed I had fewer questions, too.)

This experience also taught me that I need to ask as many legitimate questions as I can at the beginning of a project, and then, after I think it through, ask more questions if necessary. I take more careful notes, too. These habits are great time-savers; they serve both my boss and me well.

Of all the many challenging traits that bosses have, forget-fulness is probably one of the most manageable, unless blame is involved. Proactive communication-related action (such as the steps Tanya took) makes everyone's life easier, and more efficient. The steps you take to help your boss remember and follow through on commitments are also applicable to you.

TOT-Taming Tips: Forgetfulness

First of all, assess the problem. Determine if your TOT's forgetfulness results from a lack of interest in details, a preoccupation with other things, or too much focus on her own job to remember you and your work. For the boss who really can't sweat the small stuff, there are measures you can take to keep him on track and lessen your workload. You can't change your TOT's personality, but you can subtly open his eyes to consequences of his behavior and work around the trait.

 DON'T DO THIS ...

Be a Crash Dummy. Pretend you're faceless so you can be more forgettable. When your boss forgets to introduce you to a new client, even though you're standing right next to her, just stand there and smile. Practice acting like a piece of furniture—coat racks are easiest, but end tables are another option. If your boss stumbles on your name, pipe up cheerfully and say, "You can call me 'Hey you!' I also answer to 'Wotzizname.'"

Do This ...

See and Be Seen. With a forgetful TOT, your mere presence is a reminder about your departmental area and projects. Consider it "career management by walking around." While you should make yourself scarce during tantrum time, you should maximize your visibility on fit-free days. When the mood is jovial, don't hide in your office with the door shut; get out there and circulate. Pass by your TOT's door when you get coffee, or on your way back from lunch. If she is frequently forgetful, check in on a certain project during your drop-bys. It will trigger her memory, but will also position you as a concerned, interested office star.

 DON'T DO THIS ...

Hammer Your Point. Let your TOT know exactly how forgetful he is as often as possible. Every form of communication should start off with some form of "nag," such as e-mail or text messages that read: "DON'T FORGET ..." After your TOT does forget, similarly, type a follow-up message that reads: "LOOKS LIKE YOU FORGOT!" It doesn't matter if the memory lapse pertains to putting away his coffee mug in the break room, or the big client meeting he'll miss because of his conflicting jury duty. (If he blanks out on jury duty, let the judge make the point.)

Do This ...

Communicate with Style. Every interaction with your forgetful TOT is an opportunity to keep him aware of what you're working on and the input you need. If you use e-mail to communicate, use the subject line wisely. If you text message, be as brief as possible and draw attention to your longer e-mail. Use teasers that will pique his curiosity and help him remember your needs. In your voicemails and phone conversations, be cheery, positive—and concise. Have bullet points handy if you need to, and learn to communicate in bite-sized pieces. Forgetful bosses will drift off if you take too long to express yourself.

 ## DON'T DO THIS …

Use Stealth Reminders. Leave anonymous messages on her voicemail to remind her of upcoming meetings. Practice different voices, including those of well-known actors, singers, and politicians, so you can keep her from knowing your real identity. Low-tech methods can stand out. Leave notes stuck in places only she will see (on her monitor or chair, or in front of her coffee cup)—written in mysterious handwriting. Another successful approach is to have a pizza delivered to her office with the appointment time spelled out in pepperoni: "3:00 PM." If you can afford it, skywriting is very effective.

Do This …

Team Up. If the idea of online schedules, computer, and cell phone alerts are all being ignored, talk to your TOT's admin about keeping a large calendar on your TOT's desk and updating it often. Encourage the assistant to get creative with sticky notes or anything else that will call your TOT's attention to your meetings. If you have a good relationship with some of your TOT's peers, ask them to remind her of her upcoming commitments if they are involved in the same projects.

 DON'T DO THIS ...

Mimic Your TOT's Habits. Work on your side career as a stand-up comic by creating an impression of your TOT's forgetfulness. Since we know imitation is the sincerest form of flattery, be sure to imitate him all day. Try such classic gags as: walking around with his coffee cup and saying, "Has anybody seen my mug?"—or "Why are all the other department heads in the conference room—is there a meeting today?"

Do This ...

Connect Your Stuff to Bigger Stuff. Just as people use special mnemonic devices—those little mental triggers—to remember names and places, try labeling your work in ways that plainly link it to bigger projects or agendas. For example, if you know that the ultimate goal of your market analysis report is to support the company's "Global Expansion Initiative" (GEI), then name your report and refer to it in cover notes as "GEI—Market Analysis." That brand recognition will make your work seem more visible and important to your TOT—and harder to forget.

TOT-Busters Q&A

Question

My boss is constantly forgetting to tell me important things, like she made an appointment to have me meet with a manager—or that there is a conference I need to attend. I end up looking clueless. What can I do so I don't look so bad?

Answer

Begin by bringing up the issue and explaining how embarrassed this makes you feel. You don't want to be perceived as an irresponsible employee. Ask to schedule a meeting with her first thing in the morning so she can tell you about any upcoming appointments or priorities that she may otherwise forget to share with you. Encourage her to use software or Web-based solutions with shared calendars where she can enter meetings the minute she learns of them. Make sure your boss knows that you want to do well and enhance productivity. Engage her in coming up with solutions that achieve this.

 Points to Remember

- Be super-organized, patient, and forgiving, but only you can decide how much of your time should be devoted to making your boss look good (or at least not so forgetful).
- You don't need to solve the issue alone and can solicit the advice and support of others you trust.
- Most problems having to do with forgetfulness can be improved on.

- Remind, repeat, and recapture your TOT's attention.
- Make sure your TOT knows how she is affecting you, others, and the company. Get her engaged in resolving the situation—and offer to help.
- Don't take the blame for your TOT's mistakes, but do suggest positive ways to turn things around.

18

Mood Swings

About Mood Swings

YOUR NEW CLIENT is en route to your offices for an onsite meeting. It's an important gathering—the first time you and the entire client team will meet face to face. Many projects ride on this particular meeting going smoothly.

The client contact calls you from his car. His boss unexpectedly invited himself to the upcoming meeting, so he would like your boss to come along as well.

You pause. Your boss (aka your Terrible Office Tyrant—or TOT) is known for her unpredictable behavior. But since this client relationship would benefit from a meeting of the two high-ranking peers, you venture up to her office to test the waters. You float the idea of her attending the meeting and she is completely upbeat and flattered. "Great idea! Good thinking! You're doing a great job!"

You call your client back enthusiastically. You tell him proudly that your boss will be there to join everyone. He thanks you.

When the client team arrives, you escort them to the conference room and excuse yourself to let your TOT know the meeting is getting started. But instead of being jovial as she was just an hour ago, your TOT is now peevish and cranky for no apparent reason.

She pulls you aside: "Do I really need to be there? I think it does you a disservice to have me hold your hand. It'll make you look . . . helpless. But it's too late, I guess." She drags a dark cloud into the conference room.

From there, the meeting deteriorates. Both TOT bosses are whiny and carping at their underlings. You and your counterpart exchange helpless glances. In the end, no business is conducted, and both TOTs leave the room annoyed. You and your client will spend months trying to get the project back on track.

But Why?

What happened here? This meeting fell victim to a couple of classic TOT mood swings resulting in a meeting that went from a glass-half-full to glass-half-broken. Everyone experiences a sudden change of outlook from time to time, but when it comes to lightning-fast mood shifts, toddlers and TOTs truly lead the pack.

Take a look at the toddler, happy as a clam to be taken to the park, anticipating being free in the sunshine to cavort and play with his buddies. But when he arrives, he suddenly becomes whiny, clingy, and not very interested in frolicking.

TOTs can have similar unpredictable mood swings. She can be happy at one moment, then yell, "Off with their heads!" the next. Many times, you will find yourself standing in shock at the velocity of a mood change.

How are toddlers and TOTs similar in this respect?

Toddler Mood Swings	TOT Mood Swings
You're throwing a birthday party for your toddler. It's the best day of her life until it's time to open presents. One of her (soon-to-be-former) friends dares to unwrap a gift on her behalf. She bursts into tears, and declares it the "worst birt'-day ever!"	Before a major project meeting, you see your TOT in the break room. "I'm excited! The meeting is going to go well," she tells you. An hour later, she storms into the room, announcing, "This whole project is a disaster. Let's table it," and storms out.
When your friends invite your family to a family-friendly restaurant, you think your toddler *might* behave. Unfortunately, your unhappy camper uses his fries as missiles, purposely knocks over his milk, your water, and the ketchup onto the floor.	On expense report deadline day, your TOT's admin got a quick sign-off before lunch. Unfortunately, by the time you get there, she whispers, "Bad news from the big boss." Before you can dart, your TOT grabs your paperwork and barks, "I can't sign this! What were you thinking?"
Your toddler loves preschool. His teachers report he's a well-behaved little angel. You're looking forward to parent observation day. With you in the room, however, your toddler is transformed. He bites and hits his classmates, tosses action figures at the teacher's head, runs from circle time and clutches your leg screaming, "Wanna go home!"	The weekly staff meetings are a breeze until one day your TOT's boss, Big TOT, and his boss, Super TOT, sit in and observe. Your normally mellow boss becomes a raving lunatic, out to impress with authoritative style. He interrupts, shoots down proposals before the speaker is half-finished, and plays devil's advocate after every sentence.
Monday, your toddler is a dream. It is a bright sunny day, and she is all smiles. Tuesday, it rains. Your toddler now hates everything—all her toys, dolls, and books—and you. She stomps through the entire day. By bedtime, you are both ready to move out.	The stretch of grey, cold weather in February transforms your normally upbeat and reasonable boss into a nitpicking, crabby TOT. Everything you submit is bad, a waste of his time, and requires a total redo. You ponder hibernating until spring.

Why do mood swings happen? In toddlers, it's a lack of emotional maturity. They lack the experience and control to keep moods in check. If they're happy one moment and sad the next, that's fully expressed without filters to the world at large.

As human beings grow, they normally learn to manage their emotions more carefully. But not everyone makes it to adulthood with that sense of balance. TOTs can go from frolicking from cube to cube to a sudden eruption in just minutes. Working for a TOT like this can be like riding the Super Loop roller coaster. The good news is that you can develop "mood radar" with some practice. That allows you to distance yourself, and to expect the unexpected.

Unraveling Moody Mayhem

What causes mood swings?

Lack of Self-Control—Involuntary Reflex

Your TOT may be unable to regulate her responses, and, like an involuntary reflex, she just lets it rip. Afterward, she may repent privately or appear sheepish during your next encounter.

Lack of Self-Control—Voluntary Action

Sometimes, this lack of self-control is not an accident. Some TOTs may simply believe that it's their birthright to emote at will, despite any fallout, which often engenders immense fear, not to mention your lack of productivity.

Embarrassment

Mood swings can also be efforts at misdirection. A TOT who is trying to cover up his flaws, lack of knowledge, or disappointment, might engage in moodiness as a way to detract onlookers from his incompetence.

Stress

Mood swings can be brought on by outside stress factors. If your TOT is overwhelmed by personal responsibilities, financial pressures, or issues at home, then these stressors can easily bring moodiness into the office.

Chemistry

Sometimes, mood fluctuations are physiological. Parents who've waited too long to feed their kids—or who allowed too much Halloween taste-testing—know the outcome. Moods can stem from hunger to overeating to reactions to sugar or caffeine. Mood swing behavior that is more difficult to manage is based on manic or bipolar issues.

True TOT Tales

Management by Mood Swing

A bad mood swing can cause a valuable employee to resign, break a business deal, or result in a serious misjudgment affecting the direction of an entire company. Consider the experience of Alicia, a junior executive at a Southwest bank.

> *I was the point person developing a proposal for my bank. We spent untold personnel hours getting this proposal into place over a number of months. It was going to be a big step for us, if it could get enough executive support to move forward. The proposal was finally ready to be sent out. All I needed was my boss's final signature on the project budget.*

My boss was known for his mood swings and was famous for doing complete 180s on projects, proposals, and even performance evaluations, depending on his mood, and everyone knew this.

The day seemed promising at first: it was my boss's first day back from a two-week vacation. I had seen him earlier and he appeared to be in a jovial mood.

Unfortunately, things didn't proceed as I planned. While he'd been out, his e-mails had piled up, and while I thought my appointment made me first in line to see him, many people had "jumped the line" ahead of me.

When I went to his office, his admin shooed me away, saying he was "too busy. Come back later." Finally, in the early evening, my boss made time to see me. By this point, his post-vacation bliss had faded and he was grumpy and whiny.

He took one look at my proposal and went ballistic on the budget—the one he had preliminarily approved before going on vacation. There was no rhyme or reason for his reaction. And that was it. Months of work, down the drain. Plus, as the project leader, I took the heat for failing to get my superiors to sign off on the budget.

Ultimately, I learned a lesson about mood swings and timing. Since I knew my boss's mood could shift at any moment, I was wrong to assume his initial good mood would last. When I was shooed away, I should have taken that as my cue to reschedule to a day when he wasn't feeling quite so overwhelmed. Timing is everything and mine was off.

Alicia's experience was a challenging one, but instructive. She read too much into an early reading of her boss's mood-o-meter, and didn't follow her instincts. It torpedoed months of work and a lucrative project for the bank. The good news was that this experience left an indelible memory with Alicia, leading her to make more careful mood-monitoring part of her future project approval process.

TOT-Taming Tips: Mood Swings

What can be done to manage your TOT's moodiness? Since spiking his coffee with mood-altering pharmaceuticals is illegal, you'll have to try something more acceptable. Mood swings can be more manageable if you do your homework, see them coming, and are prepared.

 DON'T DO THIS . . .

Pounce. Be the first each morning to test your TOT's emotional barometer. Why get an early warning from others when you can stick *your* neck out every day? When she has just arrived at work, burst into her office with a set of items that need attention on the spot. Blurt out: "These can't wait, I need approval now!" You'll get a quick read on her mood-o-meter.

Do This . . .

Plan Your Visit. Know the best times of day to approach your boss. Is he typically upbeat in the morning? Is after lunch better—or during a coffee break? Study his patterns to determine the best times to approach him and plan your own interactions accordingly. Sometimes, the mood will swing in your favor, especially if your TOT just got a promotion, kudos from his Big TOT, a new electronic gadget, and so on. That's a great time to deal with big decisions—and bad news. The key is to know when the swings will come, and what times to make yourself available ... or scarce!

 ## DON'T DO THIS ...

Play Pretend. Proceed each day as if your TOT were the most even-tempered person on the planet. Allow your questions to pile up over a long period, so that all your requests are last minute. Act as though your TOT is one of those supervisors who is never ruffled by anything. When you ask, "Can you sign off on all my work for the past quarter?" Make sure to add a question like, "Don't tight deadlines just give you a rush?"

Do This ...

Gather Intelligence. Open a line of communication between yourself and your TOT's admin. Reach out to that person for information. What are the things that make your TOT happy? What sets her off? How can you best position yourself to avoid setting off a cycle of mood swings? The person closest to your TOT will have the best reading of the current temperature—and the long-term forecast. Offer to help out your TOT's assistant whenever you can, to show sincere gratitude for the tip-offs you get.

DON'T DO THIS ...

Imitate and Confront. You know your TOT has a 70/30 chance of being in a bad mood, so give some love back. Start your conversations with a calm "Good morning! I know you like people you can relate to, so let's play 'Unpredictable.' I'm smiling now, but I could throw a fit any second!"

Do This ...

Keep Your Cool. When your TOT's mood pendulum swings to the dark side, be a sea of calm. Remind yourself that she'll settle down soon enough. (Try reciting calming phrases like "It'll be better after lunch"—to yourself, of course!) When your TOT seems ready to sway, bring her back faster by showing a relaxed, in-control demeanor yourself. Lighten things and use distraction to "jam the system." (See Chapter 9 on *Tantrums* for more information.) Remember that her mood swings may not be about you at all—so do not take bad days personally. Finally—keep this book handy for quick relief.

 DON'T DO THIS ...

Go Over Her Head. Every time your TOT shifts from giddy to growling, complain to his boss (Big TOT). e-mails, text messages, and voicemails are okay, but nothing beats meeting one-on-one with good ol' Big TOT. Give a summary description of the current mood and the trigger for the shift each time it changes. Big TOT will surely get a kick out of these frequent reports, and your TOT will end up having fewer mood swings . . . he'll just virtually flatline at furious.

Do This . . .

Reach Out. Often mood swings are symptoms of emotional needs. While you can't be your TOT's therapist, you can offer emotional support if you have a solid, trusting relationship. Be a person your TOT can talk to as long as it doesn't interfere with your work. A system of mutual support can benefit you in your job and career. And your TOT will learn to trust and rely on you for more than just your workday output.

TOT-Busters Q&A

Question

Is it possible that my boss has a split personality? Sometimes we see two completely different versions of him, even in the same meeting. For example, yesterday's staff meeting started out badly. The boss was cranky and watching the clock. We were all thinking: This is a nightmare. But then, as the meeting wore on and people snacked, the boss's mood changed. By the end, he was upbeat, enthusiastic, even making jokes. What's happening here?

Answer

I suspect it was the cookies, coffee, or maybe both. Caffeine and sugar both generate quick energy. When they hit the bloodstream, presto, a new mood emerges. Consider providing sugary snacks at big meetings—and for extra brownie points, roll out the treats right before your part of the meeting for enthusiastic support. If the meetings will be extra long, be concise and upbeat ... but time them carefully during the day to avoid a mood-swinging sugar crash.

 Points to Remember

- Watch the clock: Know the best—and the worst—times to approach your TOT.
- Keep on an even keel, and don't let her mood swings become your mood swings.
- Consider outside triggers: What sets off a mood swing? Cookies? Late running meetings? Rainy days? Mondays?
- Get intelligence: Tap an inside source, such as your boss's admin, for tips.

19

Neediness

About Neediness

YOU'VE WORKED FOR the last six weeks on a major project that will improve the company's profitability and make you and your colleagues' jobs a lot easier. You finally reach a milestone in your project and take a moment to stare blindly into space (or at the fluorescent light above you).

Just as you begin reaching for your victory M&Ms, your Terrible Office Tyrant (TOT) appears to discuss what *he's* busy working on.

"I really nailed that McNaster account, didn't I?" he says. "Yup," you answer, but "yup" isn't enough. He's staring you down, expectantly, like a dog waiting to be petted. He wants you to comment on his brilliance, his savvy, his unprecedented boldness in getting McNaster to sign. He also makes it clear that he needs some of the candy you have on your desk.

So you make some supportive noises and he pulls up a chair, asking your opinion about how to implement the new database system, but before you can respond, he's back to McNaster again, rambling on about how hard it was to negotiate terms, how nobody had been able to close the deal before him, and so it goes until your bladder is ready to burst.

At 5:30 PM, he stands up to leave, looks at his watch and says, "Well, I'm sure you have work to do. I'd better let you get to it." Once again, he's managed to keep you in the office late, without even asking about your big project, and he wiped out your chocolate stash to boot!

But Why?

Like toddlers, TOT bosses seem to have radar that tells them when you want to be alone, and that's exactly the time they need you the most. All parents know that if they try to grab a few quiet moments, their child will suddenly appear.

Little Jody follows you to the bathroom, opening the door that you just closed, needing her shoelaces tied. When you collapse on the couch to watch your favorite show, she wants to know where babies come from or why your nose is crooked and has holes in it. Ignore her and she sticks bubble gum in the carpet or smacks you on the back repeatedly. In the same way, ignore your boss and separation anxiety is sure to set in. Instead of finding gum everywhere, though, you'll get smacked with an extra 20-page memo to draft or a lousy performance evaluation.

TOTs have no use for downtime—your downtime, that is. On the other hand, if you get too productive and busy to pay them any attention, they take it as a signal that you need refocusing—and guess where the focus needs to be? Just as little Jody demands that you watch her sock-puppet ballet when you're sitting at the desk with a stack of bills to pay, you can bet that your boss will show up in your office wanting to chat whenever you have a deadline looming.

Neediness is when TOTs want you to be excessively attentive to them. They require constant reassurance that you will take care of all their needs and deadlines. It's tricky to change because you have to balance care with setting limits. TOTs continuously need you to work by their sides, even if it means deferring your vacation or working through the weekend.

Neediness is common in human nature. When a small child cries or calls out for help, it's expected. When your boss expresses a need, it may be legitimate—or it may be a test of your boundaries. Nevertheless, you are expected to hop to it.

Let's look at situations in which toddler and TOT behavior converge:

Needy Toddler Behavior	Needy TOT Behavior
She tugs at your leg for attention when you're on the phone, incessantly whining "Mommy, Mommy, Mommy."	When you're talking to a client, your TOT barges in, barking, "I need you to redo those February projections. By noon."
As soon as it's bedtime, she becomes hungry and thirsty, chanting, "I wanna glass of water, I wanna cookie."	He becomes thirsty and hungry at 4:58 PM on Friday, and needs you to go get a drink with him, or to make a fresh pot of coffee to keep you both awake as you finish the RFP he just handed you.
Your toddler yells and screams when you try to put him in his playpen, and won't stop until you hold him.	She casts the evil eye when you mention your upcoming vacation, or slams the door when you put on your coat to leave for lunch.
Starts making "night visits" after bedtime when she gets lonely, saying, "I'm scared. My room is dark, and there are monsters. Can I stay here with you and Daddy?"	To relieve separation anxiety, your TOT starts making night visits around 6:00 PM to see who's working. "Gosh, it's quiet around here. Can I see what you're working on?"

Some bosses are born highly independent, but most require a lot of attention and reassurance. Like the toddler who wants to be king of the mountain one minute, and then wants you to feed him his sandwich in tidy bits the next, your boss fears being without subjects (meaning you) and without caretakers (yup, you again).

Separation Anxiety and Abandonment

Most toddlers develop separation anxiety at some point. They lack the assurance that things and people exist even when hidden. Your toddler clings to you and shrieks when you leave the room because she fears that you'll never come back. Likewise, your TOT fears you won't be there when her e-mail is relentless.

TOTs fear abandonment. Some TOTs can't handle it when their employees leave the building for lunch. TOTs need someone around constantly or they get frustrated with their tasks (like downloading a software update). If you leave the office or get distracted, even for an hour, they realize they may have to work alone, without your support or praise. Time off is worse. They worry that your vacation to the Rockies might inspire you to quit your job and become a full-time mountaineer.

Reassuring your TOT can be problematic, however. If you try to train your TOT to be independent by going about your own business instead of pampering her, she might resort to tirades to keep you around. (See Chapter 9 on *Tantrums* for more TOT-Taming advice.) Ironically, TOT neediness typically interferes with your ability to help.

True TOT Tales

Learnings from the Learning Center

Marta is the director of a Learning Lab at a local community college. She works for the associate dean for Academic Affairs, a particularly needy TOT.

My boss is driving me crazy. I took this job because it's a responsible, independent position and I thought I could arrange my own schedule. But the way my boss, Stephanie, treats me, I might as well be on a leash.

Yesterday afternoon, I had finished an online summary about upcoming courses by 4:30 PM and was looking forward to leaving on time, for once. At 4:45 PM, Stephanie appeared at my desk and plunked down next to me.

"What do you think of this new design for my office space?" she wanted to know, thrusting a sheaf of papers in my hand. She'd been wanting to reconfigure the Learning Center for the last year and had created one design after another. I gave her my opinion, as requested, but everything I suggested she found fault with, although she kept asking for my thoughts.

At 5:30 PM, she wanted me to walk around the building with her, go through the computer area, listen as she ranted about how the dean of the college dissed her and refused to fund her pet project. By 6:15 PM, she was still going strong. All the other staff had long since left. I looked out the window and saw flurries starting.

"Stephanie," I said, "I've got people coming for dinner, and it's starting to snow. I gotta get home."

I might as well have said, "I just set your new BMW on fire." She gave me a hostile look, turned her back to me, and walked away, muttering over her shoulder, "Well, I'll be here until at least 8:00 PM." But it worked—and I was thrilled.

It's a tightrope act working for a needy boss. You want to be available as necessary—but without compromising your own limits or sparking a retaliatory fit. If Marta had stayed at the office until 8:00 PM to appease Stephanie, she would have felt even more resentful and compromised. On the other hand, if Marta had walked out at 4:45 PM after finishing her work, Stephanie certainly would have found ways to later offset any joy Marta had in leaving early.

Marta had to do something to make the situation bearable and to preserve her time off, but what could she do? She needed the following TOT-Taming Tips to fend off her lonely boss.

TOT-Taming Tips: Neediness

Follow these Do's and Don'ts to safeguard your own sanity and independence when your TOT gets clingy.

 DON'T DO THIS …

Flaunt Your Downtime. When your boss mentions a big project looming, remind him at the last minute of your scheduled vacation by announcing something amusing like, "Well, I won't be here to help because I'll be sipping piña coladas poolside on my Caribbean cruise." You can croon about tropical breezes right after your boss gets some bad news, say, after your department gets an audit notice.

Do This …

Be Low-Key When Discussing Time Off. Ideally, send your TOT a clear, direct memo with as much advance notice as possible: "I'm planning to take two weeks off in mid-July. Will you let me know if this can be approved?" … or an e-mail or voicemail that says: "I need to take a two-hour lunch today to take care of some personal business, but I will make up the time by staying late tonight." Let your TOT know your regular schedule, too. If you have commitments on a certain night of the week, inform her that you won't be available then. Spell out how your work will be covered while you're away.

Make it clear that you won't leave loose ends behind you, and that he'll be taken care of in your absence. And always be sure to take into consideration the current economic environment, internally and externally. During tough times, this may mean temporarily sacrificing personal time to keep your job.

 ## DON'T DO THIS ...

Help Your TOT Analyze His Neediness Problem. Play psychologist and suggest to your boss that he might have developed this problem in his formative years. Be compassionate, and say "Boss, I really care about you and I observe that your inability to function on your own is hampering your career, so I've taken the liberty of contacting Dr. Whatup on your behalf. He can help you get over the trauma of early weaning so that you'll be able to write your own e-mails and even place your own calls. I know because I spent a lot of time with Dr. Whatup when that Vertex project came due. See? I'm not afraid to admit it."

Do This ...

Encourage Your TOT's Independence. Always praise your TOT when she succeeds in taking a step on her own, and remain silent when she fumbles. You want to reinforce her sense that she is a competent, able person who can thrive without your assistance. Tell her, "Thank you so much for taking that call about the family of rats living in the shipping popcorn. You do so well in handling irate customers."

 DON'T DO THIS ...

Make Yourself Too Available. If the phone rings on Saturday at 9:00 AM while your Schnauzer attempts the "sit" command during Puppy Kindergarten class, excuse yourself to take the call. It could be your TOT having yet another crisis about tangled phone cords or missing staplers. Take the call, drop the leash, and rush to the office. That way you've guaranteed a whole slew of Saturday phone calls. Make a show of how eager and available you are around the clock, so that you'll be first in line for promotion. Find out what a perfect parking space you can get at the office at 5:00 AM, and let your TOT know about it.

Do This ...

Put a Plan Together. Empathize with your TOT when there's truly a backlog: "I see how it's really putting pressure on you to have all this extra work." If it happens regularly, however, help your TOT to strategize about how to cover the load. You'll likely reinforce and encourage the idea of planning for a heavy workload in advance, and also help put limits in place.

If your TOT excessively demands your presence even when the workload doesn't require it, get over the guilt of not showing up. It won't help your TOT if you keel over from working nonstop. If you produce excellent results and do work hard, your TOT may even admire your resolve. You might even inadvertently help model it for her when she deals with her Big TOT.

 DON'T DO THIS . . .

Make Yourself Completely Indispensable. Make sure you are the person your TOT turns to for nurturing. You might beat out your colleagues for the Most Valued Overachiever Award. Make your mantra, "I can do it all myself, all of it." Never succumb to the allure of delegation to people who could replace you. When your TOT sees how well you handle the work of five people, he'll surely give you special projects so that you can do the work of 10.

Do This . . .

Wean Your TOT. Toddlers eventually learn that they can survive a night with a babysitter, and that it's fun to stay with Grandma. In the same way, you need to help your TOT learn that other people can serve him (almost) as well as you can. When your TOT overloads you, suggest someone who might help out. If your TOT bugs you all day long with nonwork-related trivial affairs, bring another colleague into the discussion. For instance, when she shows up at your cubicle trying to make a decision, say, "Gee, I can't decide. Let's ask Mike." After you direct her to Mike a number of times, he might help you out. This works particularly well if you encourage your TOT to interact with *other* needy TOTs.

TOT-Busters Q&A

Question

When my TOT is in my cubicle and my phone rings, he gets a look of utter panic. His lips quiver and sometimes there's even a tear or two. This happens whether it's an important business call or something less crucial. What should I do?

Answer

Keep in mind that a needy TOT has an overwhelming feeling of neglect. He'll hate not being the center of attention, but once he knows the call is important enough, he'll settle down. One approach is to offer that your TOT join in the conversation, on speakerphone. Usually your TOT will freeze or leave, not wanting any part of actual "work." If that fails, write a note while on the phone: "HR! Will stop by shortly!" or "The McNaster account—may have it!" You can also try handing him that report you're working on, with a bright red marker, so he can scribble and keep busy. As a last resort, offer some emergency candy out of your drawer.

Points to Remember

- Remain unapologetic when requesting time off.
- Put plans for covering work while on vacation in writing.
- Laud your TOT's successes.
- Set clear limits; determine how much overtime is necessary, and draw the line there.
- Direct your TOT to other staff members—or better yet, other TOTs.
- Establish that you are responsible and dedicated, then slowly wean your TOT by using the tips offered in this chapter.

20

Short Attention Spans

About Short Attention Spans

YOU ARE OFF-SITE with a customer, and you call to check in with your Terrible Office Tyrant (TOT) for approval. But your boss puts you on hold, on and off, for 15 minutes. Your TOT resurfaces a couple of times, but then yet another call comes in, and so you bounce back and forth with your customer, embarrassed.

When your TOT returns for a split second, you try to interject before she sentences you back to terminal hold. "Boss, this is really important," you blurt, "Mr. Stanley wants to . . .," "Uh, sorry, I have to take this," and you further endure your own company's unnerving on-hold message, "Your call is important to us . . ." Seconds later, the line goes dead.

Once more, you've had to fight for just a few minutes of uninterrupted time with your boss before something more important comes along, and you are losing the fight. You're left with questions unanswered and decisions unmade—all because you can't get your TOT to focus.

This time, connecting with your boss is critical and the clock is ticking. You have important feedback from a client—one of your best accounts. He wants to make a major budget change to your contract before things are finalized.

You stall by taking your client to lunch, and naturally, your phone rings exactly when the food arrives. Thankfully, it's your TOT: "Sorry, I couldn't get back to you before, but, oh wow, I just remembered. I've got a lunch meeting and I'm running late. We'll chat when I get back. Whatever you wanted to talk to me about, I know you can handle it."

And with that, she hangs up. This is a big budget decision, and you aren't authorized to approve that big of a change. Now what?

But Why?

You love your job; you even like your boss, but why is it so hard to get her attention? She's like a three-year-old on sugar overload. Every distraction gets her attention, until the next one pops up. That means by the end of the day you're stuck with a pile of issues that still need her attention and input. You've tried dozens of tricks to get her to focus: you've e-mailed her every hour, bribed her admin with candy to get you locked in for appointments that get cancelled at the last minute, and now you're considering sending a singing telegram.

The fact is that your TOT is exactly like a toddler when it comes to attention span. Your boss can have hundreds of distractions pop up throughout the day, just like little Ashley at dinner time. If the TV stays on or if Fido comes over to the table, poof! Ashley becomes so enamored with Fido's begging routine or what's on the tube that she loses all interest in eating.

Distracted toddlers resemble TOTs with short attention spans.

Distracted Toddler Behavior	Distracted TOT Behavior
You tell Emma she has to put her dirty clothes into the hamper before she can go outside. She picks up two items and then spots her stuffed monkey. Five minutes later, the clothes are still scattered and she's shrieking with glee, "Monkey! Monkey!"	Your boss says she can't be disturbed until she finishes typing her report, and she actually seems focused. However, 10 minutes later, you bring in useful source material that just arrived, and you see she's changing her screen saver.
Your child sits down to do his homework, but less than a minute later, he asks for juice. After that, he starts a conversation with you about ponies. Then he gets under the table to look for his pencil and finds some interesting old crackers.	When your boss is confronted with a deadline for personnel reviews, he changes the subject as often as possible. Topics include his golf game, his new haircut, and if you know how to get basketball scores on your cell phone.
You're in a hurry and try to get him to dress himself so you won't be late for the kiddie gym class, again. He runs from room to room, turning it into a game, not noticing that you're not smiling.	Your TOT brings you along so you can talk as he's heading down to his car. However, he stops at every desk along the way to "touch base." You never get to say anything except "Bye-bye."
Your child eats five chocolate cookies she got from a friend and spends the afternoon, playing "trampoline" on the sofa, her bed, your bed, and the dog.	After her third espresso, you notice that your boss is talking on her cell phone, glancing at a webinar, checking e-mail, and texting while "listening" to you.

Many TOTs with short attention spans are really only allocating a limited amount of time to each task on their plate. They know they don't have time to carefully examine everything that comes across their desks. So they've learned to scan through most information and focus only on the things that seem important—at that second.

Being thoughtful and thorough is something that a very busy boss can delegate to someone below her in the pecking order. Guess who?

Boss Attention Deficit Disorder

Of course, there are those TOTs who just have a case of Boss Attention Deficit Disorder—BADD. If this is your boss, then she's not exactly setting the world on fire with her juggling act. "So what if most of the balls hit the floor," she figures, "I'm not juggling chain-saws."

A TOT with BADD is restricted to focusing on whatever's interesting at that moment. If it's an emergency, she'll rise to the occasion. If it's not, she'll consider it until something—anything—more interesting comes along.

Many short-attention-span TOTs get obsessive over technology, especially when you're around. They use smart phones, laptops, wireless headsets, web conferencing, text messaging, and so on when you're trying to communicate face-to-face. Tools like these help TOTs give the impression that they are extraordinarily busy, in demand, and never alone. (Of course they're busy, in part, because they are perpetually trying to learn how to use all the features on their tools.)

But trying to get the attention of a gadget-laden BADD TOT is like trying to get a toddler away from his older brother's latest video game. You call his name and he turns toward you for a brief instant—maybe—and then he's "gone" again.

TOTs with limited attention spans often immobilize you and your work, causing unnecessary frustration and down time. But fortunately, there are ways to combat this trait, which will help both you and your TOT succeed in your jobs. The main one is: regaining focus.

Regaining Focus

Distractible bosses stop for every new e-mail, text, and phone chime, and every shadow that passes by their office doorway—let alone every person who walks into their offices. When your TOT loses focus that easily, it may be a sign you'll need to pitch in to help. The more you can reconnect your boss with priorities, the better off both of you will be.

If your BADD boss has never documented the primary objectives of your team on paper, you should encourage him to do so.

But you can also start small, if necessary, by checking in on a Monday morning and submitting a draft of mutual goals for the week ahead. Send them to him in an e-mail. If he starts going off-course, you can refer back to those goals. In some cases, there may be new priorities to add, but that systematic approach will keep him on track.

As the system takes hold, you can start to expand the time frame of the goals and start to bring others into the mix. You'll have a clearer sense of your responsibilities and your team will become less frazzled and more productive. And if it sounds like you're doing some of your boss's job, you are. That's another example of "managing up"—a valuable skill for TOT Tamers.

True TOT Tales

In Living Color

Anthony was moving up in his job in corporate communications. He had the education and the intelligence to rise up the ladder; all he needed was the experience. In his current job, however, much of his time was spent trying to get his boss's attention.

After only a few months on the job, I was surprised when my boss called me into her office and told me she felt I was ready to supervise the publication of our annual report. I would write the feature pieces, gather the financial data, and produce the final document, which went out to all our stockholders. I was overwhelmed by her trust in me.

I worked on the project for over a month, interviewing department heads, working with accounting, and polishing the prose.

My boss was anxious for the first draft, and I promised it for the next morning. I e-mailed the text to her first thing. To my surprise, there was no response—for days. Something was wrong. It's not like there was bad news inside. Earlier, I noticed that she had a couple of colorful reports with professional graphics and photography on her desk. Then, it struck me. Maybe she's avoiding mine because my report was all dry text, and wasn't in graphic presentation form.

With that thought, I went back to the creative designers and asked for some more help to take the visual side of the work to the next step. It took a few more days, but my boss was obviously working on other priorities. Then I packaged the text alongside the beautiful graphics and layout—printed out in full color. I proudly placed it on her desk while she was at lunch. About an hour later, she asked me to come to her office. When I walked in, she was sitting behind her desk with the report open in front of her. She was beaming and told me it was amazing.

I learned a good business lesson. The packaging of an idea is a huge part of its success or failure. And with a boss who was attention-challenged, I had to take extra measures to get my work noticed.

Anthony took his boss's lack of attention as an inspiration to change his approach for the long term. Most people want to review attention-getting, appealing material. It was an important lesson for Anthony, who later became the go-to person for great marketing packages across a variety of departments.

TOT-Taming Tips: Short Attention Spans

No matter what the reasons are for your TOT's inability to focus, your approach should always try to compensate for the problem, not make it worse. There are many ways to deal with a distracted boss and turn the problem into a positive experience. And there are many ways to make things worse. Here are some do's—and don'ts—for dealing with bosses with short attention spans.

 DON'T DO THIS ...

Hold a Stakeout. Your TOT is busy, so catch her attention when she isn't immersed with work at her desk. Just be a little creative. If she's a java fiend, spend all day in her favorite espresso bar. If you are an early bird, wait in her reserved parking space smiling with a bunch of colorful balloons, jumping up and down. You'll be able to meet her first thing in the morning if you do. If that doesn't work, blockade the lobby with a tailgate party at the end of the day, for you (and maybe others) who need a word with her.

Do This ...

Make Communications Compelling. Get to the point, but first, spend some time figuring out what the point is. Being able to summarize your thoughts and present them concisely in a powerful way are invaluable business skills. And sometimes, you need to add an incentive. Often you can get a child's attention if you offer a reward. Similarly, with your TOT you can try, "If I could have five minutes of your time right now, I won't need to touch base again until next week."

 ## DON'T DO THIS ...

Use Fuzzy Logic. Everybody loves animals. Borrow a puppy to deliver your message. Nobody can resist a golden retriever puppy. Clip your memo to the puppy's collar—and print your boss's name on the outside in large, red letters with a permanent marker. Then let the cute fuzzy thing loose into his corner office. He'll be sure to think your memo requesting two weeks off next month is "just adorable!"

Do This ...

Add a Pinch of Excitement. Try to be entertaining when you're presenting your ideas. Nobody likes a bore, and if you can't get excited about what you're doing, why should anyone else? Use props, visual aids, or any other supportive material that will keep an audience engaged in the presentation. Use humor (but skip the funny hats—and leave the pup at home).

 ## DON'T DO THIS ...

Barge in and Talk Fast. Since your TOT has a very short attention span, plan to run over to his office hourly.

If someone's already in there, don't worry, his attention will shift to you ... because when you arrive with your plea for project approvals, you'll be ready to cram a 10-page report into a lightning-fast 15 seconds (his maximum attention time). Study the fastest talkers you can ... auctioneers, used-car salesmen, and espresso drinkers. When you need sign-off, rattle this off at high speed: "Justgivemeayes-bossandI'llleaveyoualone." He may start saying yes before your 15 seconds are up.

Do This ...

Manage Interruptions. Schedule meetings, instead of barging in whenever you need something. Your boss will be better prepared and less likely to be distracted. However, you will need to reduce those potential interruptions even further. If you need your boss to review something, try to find a way to prevent outside intruders. If your meeting is critical, ask if it can be held in a nearby conference room to avoid the steady parade of coworkers that stalk her office. When appropriate, hold the meeting in your workspace instead of hers.

TOT-Busters Q&A

Question

I often go to meetings with my boss and I notice that she really has trouble staying on point. Clients sometimes ask if she's heard what they've said when she's drifted into another place. How can I help her without making it obvious to the client?

Answer

Ask your boss in advance for three key points she wants to make in any major meeting. Have an agenda prepared the day before. Review it with your boss and get feedback in advance. Spend a few minutes on the way to the meeting to discuss the strategy. If you called the meeting, begin it by stating its purpose. When the tangents start to launch at the meeting, make sure you have some great segues to bring the conversation back to the agenda, such as, "Yes, your idea will be great in the next phase of the project, under agenda item four."

 Points to Remember

- Protect your boss from distractions so that he or she can take care of business.
- Be concise.
- Stay focused on your objective. Straying from the point allows your boss more leverage to veer off as well.
- Know how to prepare an executive summary and what your boss cares about most.
- Make sure your communications are lively and interesting.
- Be vigilant. With a very busy boss, you have to watch for opportunities that will allow you to get his or her attention.

Conclusion

By NOW, YOU'VE probably recognized some of your boss's TOT-like behaviors throughout the book—and maybe some of your own, too! But more importantly, you've found a number of solutions to help ease the frustration at your job. You're now ready to be a true TOT tamer.

Remember, this is all about being professional and creative. Doing battle with a tireless TOT never works. You'll have much better results by understanding what makes managers behave like toddlers and taking a collaborative approach to resolving problems.

Of course, not every TOT is open to change, so you must also set limits. If you are in a bad or hopeless situation with your boss, it's time to regain control and move on. You can always be a TOT tamer in your next job, and if you end up with a terrific boss, that's even better.

You can make a difference at work, and you can enact change. "Managing up" will help preserve your sanity, ease the tension, and perhaps your workload. It will also make you look like a superstar in the eyes of your TOT (and maybe even Big TOT and Super TOT)—placing your career destiny back in your hands.

If your boss behaves like a Terrible Office Tyrant, by exhibiting Bratty Behavior or acting like a Little Lost Lamb, just remember: you can—and will—tame that TOT!

Special Section: Advice for Bosses—TOT Proof Your Company

IF YOU ARE a boss reading this, you are obviously an open-minded manager who understands the book's broadest value: to create a better workplace for *everyone*—even though it's very likely that you, too, have a boss. If you're a senior business leader or CEO, you may sometimes feel as if you're running an out-of-control pre-school, not a professional organization. You may be in need of fresh solutions on how to increase and sustain greater productivity, morale, and profitability, that is, how to TOT proof your company™. Regardless of how you got here, welcome to *Tame Your Terrible Office Tyrant (TOT)*.

What Is a TOT?

Although you may be concerned by the title, which includes the phrase *Terrible Office Tyrant* (TOT), this book is not about boss bashing. As a matter of fact, it's a solutions-oriented book intended to foster better relationships between managers and employees. My hope is that a little humor will help break through some barriers—and help us see the kid in all of us at the office—for a more humanized, productive, and profitable workplace.

The humorous slant might also help ease any tensions you may have with *your* boss (or difficult board members, peer managers, or clients, for example). Similarly, "terrible tyrant" is intentionally offset by "TOT," because all adults share childlike traits at some point.

What exactly is a TOT? Terrible Office Tyrants, or TOTs, are managers who can unwittingly slip into childlike behavioral modes. There are a number of striking parallels. Behaviors can range from the more aggressive category: demanding, territorial, stubborn, or tantrum-throwing—to the more benign, such as neediness, whining, fickleness, or short attention spans.

In the book, your boss is usually referred to as Big TOT, or Super TOT if he or she is your boss's boss. (The term TOT does seem funnier now when it applies to others, doesn't it?) So, now you can officially use this book to tame your own TOT, if you'll promise to collaborate with the TOT tamers reporting to you.

One of the main goals of this book is to show workers that all managers, regardless of seniority, are people, too. That makes it easier for employees to empathize with you. Overwhelmed managers, in particular, can slide right into TOTdom. Fortunately, just as there are parallels to childish behavior, there are corresponding solutions that can be applied to daily office interactions.

If you've flipped through the book, you've undoubtedly seen the term *TOT taming*. This does not refer to lion tamers with whips. TOT taming is about calm, professional, creative resolutions to challenges (which are much less painful!) In fact, a good TOT tamer will never lash out, even when she's totally exasperated by her boss.

Tame Your Terrible Office Tyrant offers employees tips on how to "manage up." This book gives you an insider's peek into the perspectives of your workforce—and what they won't tell you. So now you don't have to wish you could be a fly on the break room wall. You'll know the realities of what distracts your staff from doing their best work, and what to do about it. Eventually, that wish won't even occur to you, as you help create a TOT-free zone.

Am I a Terrible Office Tyrant?

At some point in your work life, maybe you inadvertently displayed a bout of TOT behavior. You heard the repercussions through the grapevine, staff, human resource group, or from "the top." Well, join the club—you're human. These traits transcend toddlerhood, adulthood, gender, and yes, every level in a company.

But, if after some self-reflection, you believe that a TOT unwittingly seeps into your everyday management style, kudos to you for taking action. Maybe you, like many today, are in search of a healthier bottom line for your department or firm; you want to be a better manager; or maybe you just want to keep your coveted job. They're all good reasons for change.

Now You Have the Tools

This book, and particularly this special section, will help you mitigate childish boss behavior—from a manager's standpoint. This chapter outlines how you can help make your office "safe for success" and encourage a more humanistic, productive workplace.

Chances are that throughout the workday, you swing from feeling like the boss to feeling "bossed around" yourself. Wherever you are on the pendulum, by coming here, you've taken a great step toward improving work relationships all around you. Maybe you'll become a catalyst for other managers to engage in TOT taming, as you aim to enhance the organization's profitability.

One thing is sure: you will get personal satisfaction by watching all this happen; meaning, as a manager—you, too, will *thrive* in your job.

TOT Proof Your Company

Make It Safe for Success

Did you know that:

- **More than 75 percent** of workers believe that office politics creates "harmful stress and hurts employee productivity"?
- **Over 80 percent** of workers feel that "managing up" (defined as: "being a proactive problem solver with a boss, using strong people skills, and indirectly modeling positive behaviors with their bosses") is a valuable skill that should be offered at companies—yet a whopping **70 percent** of them believe that doing so may result in getting fired?
- **91 percent** of workers believe that when bosses aren't afraid to change course *after getting employee feedback*—this action contributes to greater job satisfaction and creates a more "positive, humanistic work environment for workers." Other boss characteristics, such as being humorous, inspirational, receptive, and appreciative, received virtually equal votes—between 91 and 94 percent.

These findings are part of a March 2008 U.S. study of 586 workers aged 18 years and older, commissioned by Lynn Taylor Consulting and conducted by an independent global research firm.

As a CEO or senior manager, you wield tremendous influence to seize the opportunities presented here—to create an exuberant workforce and increase profitability.

Are your team members free to explore new innovations; take calculated risks; and continually expand their contributions? You can decide whether your organization is ready to be safe for success.

However, if you have TOTs running amok in your company, they're not leaving visible trails of juice stains or chocolate down the hallway. You are often made aware of their stifling ways only *after* they've left the company—and you've opened the floodgates of information.

Simply stated, TOTs who impede the growth or well-being of your employees are putting your profits in peril and should not be tolerated. You must TOT proof your company if you want to remain competitive.

A Comparative Look

Child-proofing a home, as you know, makes it safe for your kids to run about freely, explore, and learn. It certainly creates a less worrisome environment for those in charge of the household. Some consider babysitters a form of child proofing, so let's use that humanistic definition in the following analogy.

Two-year-old Celia, who's been getting lots of attention lately, sees her seven-year-old brother Jared's new, bright-colored box of clay on the carpeted stairway. She crawls down to get it as she beams, "Yay, clay!" Jared is on "10-minute babysitting duty," but by the time he notices, his prized clay is already in possession. Irritated, Jared just watches defiantly as Celia wobbles and then rolls down the last couple of steps. She cries, and the mood causes a chain reaction in the family. Jared quietly retrieves the clay.

Cut to a boardroom meeting. Celia, a middle manager, has the seed of a great innovation that will improve the bottom line. Others listen with interest. But Celia's boss, Jared, is a petty and territorial TOT who sees that idea as his domain. He interrupts, and after the meeting, says to Celia, "Yeah, that idea won't fly. By the way, I have a couple projects for you. See me after lunch." Celia's morale sinks, which spreads among others over time, as Jared continues to focus on his own interests, not the company's.

Unfortunately, TOT-attacks, subversive and blatant, go on all day under the radar of managers at all levels, due to fear of reprisal—creating fear of failure *and* success. Stories like this make most CEOs and senior managers cringe. But it takes proactive sleuthing on your part to uncover them and to TOT proof your company.

Whether TOT proofing or child proofing, both allay worry on your part because you know that the environment will be *safe for success*. It allows workers to be their best, which directly leads to greater efficiency . . . and a more attractive balance sheet.

P.S. We all know child proof doesn't mean get rid of your child. But if *corporate* TOTs refuse to be tamed, it may well be time to show them the door.

You Are the Role Model

"We must become the change we want to see" are the words of Mahatma Gandhi. This timeless phrase couldn't be truer in the world of business. To mitigate TOT behavior among your managers, you must be the role model your managers look up to and emulate. Not convinced?

TOTs on overdrive and toddlers tend to constantly mimic authority figures. In *both* cases, this manifests itself in everything from how they dress and walk to how they talk. Even non-TOTs take their cue from you, but thankfully, they are not all mirror images and can think independently.

So if you "model" the suggestions outlined in the Tips section, found later in this chapter, your managers will soon play "follow the leader."

Adopt a "No TOT" Tolerance Policy

Why must there be a "no TOT" tolerance policy in today's competitive marketplace? Because anything that hurts morale is not just morally wrong, it also deters you from focusing on winning.

There's a wealth of statistics on the cost of turnover, absenteeism, and retraining . . . and the expense is staggering. But the less discernible costs of having "TOTs on Board" are: the numbers of customers you're losing or not acquiring due an unmotivated staff; the impending loss of your best people, and signals to prospective hires and vendors through word of mouth that your managers are second rate.

If you have demanding, territorial, stubborn, incapable, or indecisive managers, your business is not operating at full throttle. Our independent studies show that most employees quietly go about their business, producing what they can, but will not speak up for fear of reprisal. If you have TOTs on your management team, you may be breeding a small army of troublesome toddlers in your company.

And when bosses are in over their heads, they can become fearful little children, afraid to make mistakes or anxious about a certain outcome. That has a ripple effect on their team members. Executives should be on alert for the "TOTometer" in them and their less senior managers.

Humanize Your Workplace™

A collaborative work environment in which everyone puts the larger good of the company first is the flip side of a corporate playground rampant with "TOTren!" It may seem like a desert mirage, but it is actually more attainable than it appears. To "humanize your workplace," you must elicit cooperation from all sides. With diligence and consistency, it is possible.

Humanizing the workplace includes a broad range of actions, but can include:

- Deliberately trying to read people more accurately;
- Inspiring your team;
- Creating a family feeling in your company;
- Allowing something as simple as humor—"the great diffuser"—as I call it, to enter into a tense discussion.
- Having common goals of communication, motivation, and respect between manager and employee.

It isn't altruistic or even about thriving in your job. It's bigger: it's about *your company thriving*.

Let's take a look at a senior manager's personal journey with his own TOT manager.

True TOT Tales

One TOT's Reign of Terror

Tom was an executive vice president at a growing health care services company with offices across the country. He was tasked with overseeing the expansion plans of each region, and he usually made one visit per quarter to each location. Each office had its own challenges, but overall, he was impressed with his teams.

He especially looked forward to his visits to the Northwest. The team there was always respectful and professional, and was a relief from the frenetic pace of many of the other locations. Cynthia, the regional manager in Seattle, was always on the ball, and seemed like a rising star in the company. Tom tried to encourage the other teams to work a little more like her group.

However, when the year-end reports were compiled, Tom was shocked to see the Seattle office's numbers in a free fall. Revenues were down, client retention was terrible, and complaints were sky-high. This "model" division was a train wreck.

Tom flew into town and walked into the office. Cynthia had flown the coop. "It looked like a postapocalyptic nightmare," Tom said. "People were wandering around dazed, and Cynthia's office was trashed." Someone approached me and asked, 'Are you here to fire us?' "

Apparently, Cynthia had launched into a major tantrum after a call with Tom, storming through the office, blaming everyone for the poor numbers, and claiming that their office was going to be shut down. That lasted for two days and then she stopped coming into the office.

Tom described the rest of the saga as follows:

> After I assured everyone that Seattle wasn't closing, the team began sharing horror stories with me. Cynthia was a bully, cracking down on people who didn't do everything exactly as she wanted. She hated noise, so she apparently used a white noise machine to tune out others. She also enforced a "silence is golden" policy. That's why the office was always so quiet and what I thought was professional!
>
> Cynthia was so fearful about letting her expenses go over budget that she wouldn't let her team spend any money to address client problems. Our customers got so irritated that they walked out on us, in droves. Cynthia had hired great people, but she wouldn't let them be creative or customer-focused.

I decided on the spot to take over Seattle in the interim. I was soon overwhelmed with ideas from the team on how to repair the damage. I realized that if I focused on internal rebuilding, the group could help reestablish a strong customer base. About six months later, the region was on track to be one of our most profitable, and I turned it over to a senior account rep who was a positive, warm, and driven person.

Thousands of poor business decisions are being made every day, based on saving face, protecting sandboxes, and eggshell egos. A bullying boss like Cynthia spent so much time imposing her will that she stopped considering what was right for customers. Even worse, she created an environment where employees didn't feel safe—or motivated—to help build the company.

Unfortunately, there are many TOTs like Cynthia. The stories are endless. Billion-dollar mergers have fallen apart; military airplanes have crashed; and multimillion dollar start-ups have never gotten off the ground, due to TOT executives who were too focused on "what's in it for me."

Fortunately, there are many ways to deal with TOT managers that will make corporate life seem more like a visit to a team-oriented family than to an unruly schoolyard.

TOT-Proofing Tips

By TOT proofing your company, you can create a win-win-win, for your managers, your employees, and your bottom line, by taking charge—and making it safe for success.

Throughout the book, I've shared ideas with employees on how to deal with TOT behavior exhibited by their bosses. Those tips are valid for you, too, but as a company leader, you have more options. Here are some Do's and Don'ts, starting with the Don'ts:

DON'T DO THIS …

Avoid Employees. You're a busy executive. Don't waste your time talking to the rank-and-file. Get your "411" directly from other managers. Better yet, read it in a "one-paragraph only" mandated e-mail or two-line text message. The less time, the fewer hassles. And you won't have to drink break room coffee or worry about catching someone's cold.

Do This …

Keep Your Ear to the Ground. It would be wonderful if everything you needed to know about your company came neatly in a one-page e-mail, but your business is probably more complex. You've got to talk to your employees. Not only are you going to get insights from the people who are closest to your customers, but also you'll get a balanced look at how your managers do business. You just might uncover problems early.

When dealing with a childish boss, many employees have little choice but to endure the tirades, incessant questions, impulsiveness, and hair-trigger mood swings that are shared daily. Consider structured programs that monitor management styles, and solicit feedback from subordinates.

 DON'T DO THIS …

Give Your Managers Free Rein. If you've hired people to manage, let 'em manage. If they passed muster during the interview, they're ready to make good things happen forever more. You can trust them. After all, *you* hired them.

Do This . . .

Guide Your Managers. While it's true that you should have faith in your managers to do a good job, they need (and crave) guidance. Make sure you are setting expectations and clear goals for your team—and that you coach them regularly. If you create benchmarks for success, working with your human resources team, you can track how they are performing. But be sure to include benchmarks that address employee feedback.

If turnover or absenteeism problems surface, do an "audit" of your management team just as you would with your financials. You may discover that you have some TOTs in your midst. You may need to have frank discussions, explore management training, mentoring, coaching, and if necessary, give verbal or written warnings.

 DON'T DO THIS . . .

Hire Hot Shots. When interviewing for an open manager's slot, prepare to be dazzled. You want the fastest-talking, best-dressed show ponies out there. If you're impressed, just imagine how your employees will feel.

Do This . . .

Balance Energy and Empathy. There's nothing wrong with energy and enthusiasm in new hires. In fact, it's great. However, you'll need a lot more than that when they're on the job, especially if the job has less to do with sales, and more to do with managing others.

Hire managers who demonstrate sound judgment when you ask them hypothetical questions in the interview process. You want managers who are good listeners and problem solvers. A good manager will inspire and motivate but also spot obstacles and negative trends early. When interviewing, ask how the prospective manager led a *group* of people to great accomplishments, not about the applicant's individual track record.

And while promoting from within is highly motivational, sometimes the best person may exist on the outside (which may not be the path of least resistance). Tap into your human resource team to ensure you have all the tools and resources you need.

 DON'T DO THIS ...

Go on a TOT Witch Hunt. If TOTs are everywhere, your company must be absolutely infested with them. Assume every manager in your organization is a Terrible Office Tyrant and build a giant crib for all of them. Order a case of pacifiers and put warm milk in the coffeemaker. Draw the line at changing diapers, though. You may end up violating labor laws.

Do This ...

Be a Concerned "Parent." TOTs *are* everywhere, but typically, many cases of TOT-itis are minor and treatable. Instead of overreacting to TOT behavior, simply be on the lookout. If you observe managers acting irrationally, spend a little time understanding why. TOT behaviors are often amplified by stress. Is there something unusual affecting this person? If you can help them work through the issue, then you'll probably also have a positive impact on others, too.

Make sure not to play favorites. You can't let TOT behavior continue in someone just because he's your pal—or she's a sales leader. Address conflicts early, and begin working with the managers to address problem traits. Sometimes you can't change the person, and you must change the personnel.

 DON'T DO THIS . . .

Give Yourself a "Get Out of Timeout Free" Card. Don't worry about your own behavior. You've got to focus on the TOTs running loose in your company. You've read the book, so you're absolutely fine.

Do This . . .

Give Yourself a Check Up. Everyone has a little TOT inside them. Maybe that includes you. (Okay, if you've never ignored an e-mail, felt threatened by change, or acted on a whim, you can skip this one.) In order to TOT proof your company, start with you. Skim the table of contents and ask yourself, "Have I ever done this?" Once you're aware of a behavior, take honest steps to self-correct it. As a leader, you should also invest time in coaching and mentoring your people on the best ways to manage their employees.

DON'T DO THIS ...

Never Count on Others for the Big Stuff. It's a well-known fact that you can only rely on yourself to get anything done right. So why roll the dice on something as important as "strategy" and watch your company go down the tubes? Remember this handy new phrase for anything important: "If you must delegate, then interrogate."

Do This ...

Let Managers Shine. Winston Churchill said, "Give us the tools, and we will finish the job." No matter what level at a company, all those who receive paychecks want to be part of your goals in one form or another. And that's only to your benefit. It is easy to forget that your managers take pride in developing solutions with the least amount of prodding or micromanaging. The more you observe your managers asking, "So then, you'd like me to proceed with this idea?" and you approve—know that you may increasingly anoint yourself the preeminent anti-TOT.

TOT-Proofing Checklist

☐ **Declare Your Company a TOT-Free Zone.** The fun, light-hearted side of a child is something that can inspire us to be creative and humorous. But allowing TOTs to rule the day won't work. Introduce your team to the idea of the Terrible Office Tyrant, and let them know that TOT behavior is a no-go in your organization. Help them understand that while everyone has a little TOT in them, it can—and must—be tamed. Give employees a platform to raise their concerns about TOT bosses and share ideas about how to spot a TOT—and deal with the behavior.

☐ **Actively Seek Feedback.** Encourage input, and recognize that sometimes feedback needs to be guaranteed to be confidential. Always get informal report cards on your managers as you do on other aspects of the business. Don't wait until you start getting lots of poor reports. Talk to your team—and customers—regularly. Your people are on the front lines and are your richest resource.

☐ **Build Trust.** If you're getting out of your office enough, you've already gained your employees' trust. If you haven't, prepare to invest the time and effort to build it. Make yourself available. Ask questions and demonstrate that you care about their concerns and ideas. If you've earned their confidence, you'll get an invaluable picture of who your managers are. Over time, the resolution will become high-definition.

☐ **Open Communication Channels.** You can't fix problems if you never hear about them. However, most employees who struggle with TOTs feel that they must remain silent. Avoid creating an environment where no one feels they can speak up. Make sure you've created a safe haven for employees who need to report TOT behavior, whether it's your office, human resources, or both.

☐ **Confront Issues Directly.** Don't avoid the conflict hoping it will disappear. Address the source. There is a domino effect when your management wields power and is feared. Bring people together. Don't encourage divisiveness. Give everyone a chance to speak briefly about their perspective. There are always two sides. Show that you care; it's contagious.

☐ **Look Beyond Charm.** There are some managers who are lovely charmers when they're around you. But turn your head, and because they fear for their jobs—they have their assistants jumping through endless hoops, trying to please them and, ultimately, you. In the end, no one is pleased.

- ☐ **Humanize Criticism:**
  - ☐ Identify issues clearly and concisely.
  - ☐ Be an active listener and restate problems as others describe them to you.
  - ☐ Couch criticism in a way than spurs positive changes, and remember to wrap the negative with constructive, positive feedback.
  - ☐ Try to avoid the use of "You" statements; use "I" statements, which are less inflammatory.
  - ☐ Be calm, patient, and use humor to relax the person, where possible.
  - ☐ Remain open-minded to the other person's views.
  - ☐ Reinforce positive change, even if it's a small improvement, and remind employees how important their can-do attitude is to you and to the company.
  - ☐ Praise often. "Kind words can be short and easy to speak, but their echoes are truly endless," said Mother Teresa, but the phrase applies powerfully to employees.
  - ☐ Always hold respect as a cornerstone in your organization.
  - ☐ Provide feedback often.

And again, if you are still reading this, it's clear you are interested in improving. So . . . congratulations on looking at a new view toward enhancing your business—taming your TOT!

 Points to Remember

- ▪ "To TOT is human" but if it's a common theme, change is needed.
- ▪ Just as you would child-proof a home, TOT proof your company.

- You and your managers are role models. Be the change you want emulated.
- As a boss or CEO, if you tame TOT behavior, you'll create a win-win-win, for you, your employees, and the company.
- Humanize your workplace, and watch productivity soar.
- Make your company safe for success.
- Take action now, but remember, it's an ongoing process for you *and* your managers.
- Most importantly, a TOT-free company is a profitable company.

As a leader in your organization, you have unique power to stop petty, costly, territorial, and face-saving maneuvers in their tracks. Don't allow childish behavior to sap your employees of the very two things you want from most from them ... loyalty and great contributions.

What are the costs of *not* dealing with the TOT factor? For one, your job could be at stake. If you have many TOTs in your company, your firm could crumble because at the end of the day, we all report to someone, be it customers, boards, or shareholders. Ultimately, poor or childish managers are synonymous with poor results.

You *can* create: an environment that champions invigorating ideas and common goals ... a fertile ground for working *together*, not at odds ... a place that keeps and attracts the best people, meaning more customers, and a healthier bottom line.

You *can* TOT proof your company!

About Lynn Taylor

LYNN TAYLOR is a leading national expert and spokesperson on career, hiring, and workplace subjects. She serves as an advisor to job seekers and employees, as well as to executives on employment and motivational issues. Taylor has developed her insights on successfully dealing with difficult bosses into the Terrible Office Tyrant (TOT) franchise, which includes the book, *Tame Your Terrible Office Tyrant*™, additional books, merchandise, online media, and other projects.

Taylor's Tame Your TOT online community site is at: www.tameyourTOT.com and is a regular destination for employees seeking help with career development, office politics, managing up, dealing with difficult bosses, and corporate culture.

As CEO of Lynn Taylor Consulting, Taylor offers solutions to organizations on how to motivate teams and increase productivity through a more dedicated workforce. Employers embrace her programs, such as how to Humanize Your Workplace™ and TOT Proof Your Company, through consulting, speeches, and workshops, which incorporate her firm's ongoing research findings. For more information, visit LynnTaylorConsulting.com.

Taylor's 20 years of workplace expertise is rooted in her own corporate experience, including executive and advisory roles with two global employment firms. She has been a major contributor to several widely acclaimed books on careers, human resources, and hiring.

Taylor has been quoted extensively in hundreds of media outlets as a respected analyst of ongoing workplace studies—including *BusinessWeek, The Wall Street Journal, Fortune, The New York Times, USA Today,* and *Glamour,* and interviewed for countless broadcast news features.

Her quotations are also featured in: *If My Career's on the Fast Track, Where Do I Get a Road Map?* (Anne Fisher, New York: Harper Perennial, 2002); *Great Leaders See the Future First* (Carolyn Corbin, Washington, D.C.: Dearborn Trade, 2000); and *Generations at Work* (Ron Zemke et al., New York: AMACOM, 1999).

Lynn Taylor is a member of the National Association of Women Business Owners (NAWBO), Society for Human Resource Management (SHRM), National Association for Female Executives (NAFE), and is active with various national charitable organizations. She received her BA in Journalism and Mass Communications from New York University.

Index